G000082751

Oh No! It's Local Rock and Roll

...but I like it!

Oh No! It's Local Rock and Roll

...but I like it!

**A FOND LOOK BACK AT THE ROOTS OF
ROCK AND ROLL IN TAUNTON AND SOUTH SOMERSET
1959–1979**

Barry Sowden

HALSGROVE

First published in Great Britain in 2004

British Library Cataloguing-in-Publication Data
A CIP record for this title is available from the British Library

ISBN 1 84114 397 9

HALSGROVE

Halsgrove House
Lower Moor Way
Tiverton, Devon EX16 6SS
Tel: 01884 243242
Fax: 01884 243325
email: sales@halsgrove.com
website: www.halsgrove.com

Printed and bound in Great Britain by CPI Bath Press, Bath

Contents

For Connor and Caitlin

Foreword

This is the third book in the series *Oh No! It's Local Rock and Roll... but I like it!* The first, published in 2002, chronicled the shenanigans of musicians from Tiverton and mid Devon. The second, published in 2003, revealed the successes and secrets of the bands from Exeter and East Devon. This book uncovers the Taunton and South Somerset scene. At this rate, it looks like the author, Barry Sowden, will be still scribbling away at home in Tiverton whilst his ever-tolerant wife, Mary, is out collecting his pension!

Of course pension-collecting is not in the frame for Barry just yet, and in the meantime he makes do with collecting other things – all sorts of things – like old radios, for example, and old record players – and yes, they all still work! Barry writes in a room surrounded by his various collections – and a very large working jukebox – and an even larger Pepsi vending machine. Although this still lights up, it no longer dispenses Pepsi. Barry has converted it into a huge cupboard to house yet more of his collections.

Pride of place, of course, goes to his extensive collection of musical instruments. Saxophones, trumpets and trombones mingle with guitars, banjos, mandolins and even a pedal steel, and there are keyboards and violins in abundance – all of which Barry can play! Oh! did I mention the bagpipes? He can play them too! But, of course, Barry is most at home with his much-loved Fender Stratocaster. It's not so much an instrument, it's more like an extension of his body – he is a superb player.

As well as being an enthusiastic collector, Barry is an addict. Nothing nasty, just tea, which he can consume, unaided, in considerable quantities. If he calls on you when he is researching his next book, put the kettle on quick! Barry has the enviable knack of meeting people, drawing out their anecdotes and marrying these to long-forgotten photographs, programmes and posters. His books are a delight to musicians and fans alike, for they remind us all of the days when we were young, and were having some of the best times of our lives. Thank you, Barry.

Finally, take care! Barry's books are very readable. His easy storytelling style is deceptive. You can start out just dipping in, then may well end up hooked, and reading this book from cover to cover. Still, don't worry, the really good news is that you can always go back and read about your favourite bands again and again... and again!

OK, so having read the above, you may well be asking what is an Exeter musician doing, writing the Foreword to a book about Taunton and South Somerset musicians? Well, about eighteen months ago I bought Barry's first book. I loved it! Lots of musicians I knew had talked about such a project, but this man, Barry Sowden, had got his act together and had actually done it. Amazing! When I heard he was writing a second book, about Exeter and East Devon musicians, I sent him a few jottings about the bands which I had played with over the years, and that started it all. With Barry's encouragement I contacted some old friends who had played with me thirty-five years ago in The Son Set. Together, we reformed the band to play at the launch of his second book… and we've kept on playing because it's fun!

We hope some of the Taunton and South Somerset bands will do the same!

Alan Haydon
Saxophonist
2004

Alan Haydon.

Acknowledgements

Julie and Pete Bealey, Dave Beck, Shirley and John Beer, Brian Blackmore, Judi and Alan Boobyer, Gerry and Keith Boobyer, Paula and Derek Bristow, Dave Buckley, Witold Budzynsky, Tony Byrne-Jones, Penny and Alan Chard, Theresa and Garry Chard, Tony Charman, Celia and Dave Clapperton, Jen and Bob Conibeer, Sue and Phil Crick, Selina and Rod Cork, Stella and Grahame Darch, Jean and Ray Denning, Kevin Dunn, Steve Edwards, Ron Fellows, Julie and James Field, Shaun Gillman, Midge and Dave Greedy, Judy and Mike Green, Andy Greer, Bill Hadley, Richard Harris, Graham Hart, Tina and Dennis Hawker, Maureen and Alan Haydon, Maggie Hemming, Alan Horn, Jean and Frank Huddy, Phil Hyde, Sally and Steve Hyde, Dave 'The Rave' Illingworth, Peter Ingram, Bob 'BJ' Jarvis, Jim Knight, Peter Lee, Carole, Brian and Simon Mapstone, Val and Ian 'Butch' May, Wendy and Keith Miller, Tony Paisley, Doug Parish, Chris Perrin, Valerie Pile, Andrew Priddy, Mike Ray, Penny and Charlie Salter, Nola and Steve Stimpson, Dave Stratford, Alison and John Tingay, Trevor Trevelyan, Sharon and Steve Tucker, Dave Wheadon, Marilyn White, Jane and John Wilmington.

SPECIAL THANKS

I welcome the opportunity to offer my respect, affection and gratitude to Dave 'Dan'l' Wood for his assistance with the research and photographic elements of this book. Additionally, I am indebted to the nursing staff of the Emergency Medical Unit and Avon ward at the Royal Devon & Exeter Hospital, Wonford. My thanks are quite literally, heartfelt!

And finally to three gentlemen whose company, given the circumstances and surroundings, I thoroughly enjoyed at the latter end of June this year, for their encouragement and kindness: Dave 'Mo' Morris the jigsaw champion, Peter the steam engine enthusiast, and Ralph. I sincerely hope that your recovery is both rapid and complete.

Dave 'Dan'l' Wood.

MUM AND DAD

Whilst conducting an interview with a guitarist from the Chard area during the research of this book, the conversation was pleasantly interrupted by the arrival of his daughter and nine-year-old grandson.

Upon being introduced, and after politely shaking hands with Dan'l Wood and myself, the strapping youngster greeted his grandfather with a hug and asked, 'Is it all right to have a go on your guitar grandad?'

'You carry on lad,' the musician replied with a smile.

I watched with interest as the boy removed his coat. 'You've got to take your coat off,' he explained, 'otherwise the zip might scratch the back of the guitar, and grandad would go up the wall.'

'Quite right too,' said Dan'l.

The boy walked to the corner of the lounge and lifted the Gibson 'Les Paul' Custom guitar from its stand. Perching himself precariously upon the very edge of the sofa, he proceeded, albeit hesitantly, to play the opening bars of the Shadows classic instrumental 'Apache'.

'Very good,' I ventured. 'Keep practising, and you'll soon be as good as your grandad.'

'I practise every day,' he said solemnly. 'But this guitar's a bit heavy for me, I'd rather have my Fender – well, it's not really a Fender – it's a Squire, but it does say Fender on the top.'

'Did you save up for it?' I enquired. 'Or was it a present?'

'Actually,' he replied, 'Dad bought it for me and he says that I've got to pay him back but I know he doesn't mean it, he never does.'

The love bestowed by parents upon their children is unconditional.

Thank you Mum and Dad.

A TRIBUTE TO BRIAN MAPSTONE

This book would be incomplete if reference were not made to a man who has doubtless done more to champion the cause of music and musicians in Somerset than any other.

Born in Street on 20 April 1941, Frederick Henry Brian Mapstone, or Brian as he is more familiarly known, lived with his parents in a large mobile home on a residential park called The Homestead of which his father was the caretaker. Given a guitar as a present on his eleventh birthday, he had mastered all the essential chords by the time that he became a pupil at Wells Blue Grammar School. Subsequently, together with Mike Argent who also lived at The Homestead, and two friends, Dave Wait and Ian Steinson,who lived in Wookey and whom he had met at the youth club, Brian formed a skiffle group rather aptly named The Homesteaders.

Brian was taught at an early age to appreciate the value of money. He quickly realised that, other than his parents and relatives and on special occasions like birthdays and at Christmas, nobody actually gave you money, it had to be earned. At the age of fifteen, he started work on a part-time basis on Saturdays and during the school holidays, at the Lower Milton Dairies near Wookey which were owned by a lady called Mrs Ruff. The work was varied, and Brian thought it infinitely preferable to a paper round. The main attraction at the dairy as far as Brian was concerned, however, was Mrs Ruff's niece, Carole. A pretty and intelligent girl, Carole looked after the company's books and Brian was instantly smitten with her. Many months passed before he plucked up sufficient courage to ask the young lady out, but he was thrilled when, on the eve of her sixteenth birthday, she accepted his invitation to accompany him to Priddy Fair. After a lengthy courtship – rivalled only by a council worker's tea break – Carole and Brian became engaged. Miss Carole Anne Green finally became Mrs Mapstone on 28 July 1962.

Meanwhile, Brian had left school in 1958 and secured employment as a management trainee in the pattern-cutting and design department of Clarkes Footwear. Travelling daily from Wookey to Street on his Lambretta scooter, Brian enjoyed the job immensely.

Weekends were of course special, Saturdays in particular, when he took the stage with The Salvoes (see the biography of Eddie Dark and The Salvoes later in this book). Brian began promoting his own dances in 1963, and the following year he met the man who was to become a lifelong friend and partner in many of his enterprises, Garth Muton. In the course of his work

Brian Mapstone at Glaston-bury Town Hall.

For better or for worse: l–r: Dave Wait, Ian Stein, Brian, Carole, Mike Argent, Eddy Dark (Ron Fellows).

Brian and Carole at The Homestead, Wookey Hole.

The interior of Westside Music at Weston-super-Mare.

as a progress-chaser at Clarkes Footwear, Garth often came into contact with Brian. In conversation over lunch in the factory canteen, the two young men discovered that they shared a love of music, and Garth's offer to assist at Brian's homespun dances could not have been more sincere. Garth was able to shoulder the administrative burden, which allowed Brian the freedom to work with, and on behalf of, the musicians and the general public.

The name Westside Promotions evolved from one of Carole Mapstone's favourite musicals, West Side Story. Garth and Brian had previously considered Western Promotions, but decided that the name sounded too much like a football pools company. Initially hiring village halls in the Street and Glastonbury area – and always using local bands – Westside-promoted dances were a major triumph, to the extent that the small buildings simply did not have the capacity to meet the demand. Larger venues were sought and found. By arrangement with the respective town councils, Westside Promotions were afforded the regular letting of both Street and Glastonbury Town Halls. The lucky dance-going people of Somerset were treated to live music from top-flight acts such as T. Rex, Alexis Korner and Fleetwood Mac at Glastonbury Town Hall, thanks to Brian Mapstone and, as previously stated, local bands were invariably booked to support the professionals. It is well to note that Brian's wife Carole demonstrated her support and faith in her husband's business acumen, by manning the cash desk and simultaneously keeping a weather-eye on their year-old-son, Simon, who usually slept unconcerned in his carrycot, strategically placed at his mother's feet.

Brian and Garth left the employ of Clarkes Footwear during 1964, to devote all their energies to Westside Promotions. An office was opened in Street at the junction of Farm Road and the High Street, and the business prospered. Other joint ventures were the purchase of a recording studio in Shepton Mallet and a shop in Street, which specialised in fabric of all types. The shop – M&M Fabrics, was managed by Garth's wife Ann – and formed part of the settlement when the partnership, though not the friendship, of Garth and Brian was dissolved.

Brian retained the promotional side of the business, and continued to operate from the ground-level office in Street. Purely as an 'eye-catcher', Brian placed his Burns guitar and amplifier in the window and was surprised when a gentleman entered the office and enquired of the cost of the two items. Thinking on the run, Brian quoted what he thought was a fair price and was rendered almost speechless when the gentleman produced a handful of five pound notes and paid for the goods without question.

This spontaneous near comical incident fuelled Brian's thoughts and marked the beginning of Westside Music. A telephone call to a musical instrument dealer Duck, Son & Pinker in Bath, resulted in Brian purchasing a large quantity of repossessed instruments and musical equipment. Additionally, Jack Winstanley, the manager of the warehouse, was able to furnish Brian with much useful information regarding wholesale purchasing and the like.

The Street office became Westside Music and ran, conveniently, in tandem with the promotional side of the business. Experienced and novice musicians visited the shop in numbers. Managers and roadies, even wives whose guitarist husbands had just popped in to try out the latest model Fender or Gibson and were hours late for their dinner, could frequently be found at the shop.

During the next five years, the name Westside Music was also to be seen adorning the frontage of shops in Bridgwater, Yeovil and Bath. On the death of his father, Brian brought his mother Kathleen into the business by acquiring a tobacconist and newsagents in Street. Kath was installed as the manageress of B&K Mapstone, and lived in the flat above the shop. But as any businessman will confirm, if you see a light at the end of the tunnel, it's probably a bailiff's torch. Rising interest rates, taxation on practically everything from profits to bed-wetting, and the decline in live music all had a profound effect on Westside Music and its promotional wing. Fair-weather bank managers – whose smiles seemed to broaden and diminish in direct proportion to the size of the Westside account – suddenly began to invite Brian in 'for a little chat'.

In a combined cost-cutting and consolidation review of the business as a whole, Brian pored agonisingly over the year's trading accounts. At the end of the 'very generous' seven days' respite period granted by his bank, he knew in his own mind that Westside Music would continue to trade. The music shop in Bath was sold, as was the newsagents. For a short time, the Farm Road premises in Street became a craft and gift shop with Kathleen as its manager, but it eventually reverted back to a music shop. The recording studio at Shepton Mallet was closed down and a second mortgage taken out on his own home.

In 1971, Westside Promotions were taken over by Nick Mills. A polio victim and former accounts clerk with Clarkes Footwear, Nick is currently believed to be living in Canada, and still involved in the music industry.

Brian threw all his business knowledge and energies into the shops in Street, Bridgwater and Yeovil, and Carole, a partner in the truest sense of the word and an absolute pillar of strength throughout the difficult days, donned the mantle of company secretary in addition to her duties as a mother and shop assistant.

Brian and Carole were thrilled when, at the age of sixteen, their eldest son Simon expressed a wish to join the business. Educated at the Cathedral School in Wells, Simon had been an exceptional pupil. A member of the Cathedral choir, he had learned to play the trumpet and had taken keyboard lessons with a gentleman called Ken Sherring who lived in Yeovil.

'Time Out' for the Mapstones.

On 14 October 1971, his seventeenth birthday, Simon was presented with his provisional driving licence. He passed his driving test at the first attempt just two months later and, after a brief period of familiarisation on the quieter roads of Somerset, could often be seen in the London area collecting and delivering organs and pianos, in the company's Luton van. When not on the road, serving in the shop or making the tea, Simon helped Dave Goodway, the electronics engineer. Dave carried out the repairs to amplifiers, echo units, speakers and foot-switches etc. and was pleased to pass his knowledge on to his ever-willing assistant.

Brian opened a shop at 24 Bridge Street in Taunton in 1987, prompted by the closure of both Minn's and City Music in the town. The available floor space was subsequently doubled when he acquired the adjoining premises at number 26. With the opening of the Weston-super-Mare branch of Westside Music in 1999, the Bridgwater shop was sold to a local greengrocer and the Yeovil branch was sold in 2003.

The upper floors of the Taunton branch were converted to lecture rooms and studios, and there are currently three hundred students registered with the fourteen professional tutors who teach there. Tuition is available to would-be drummers, piano and keyboard players, guitarists, bass players and singers. Brian and Carole, together with Simon, now a full partner in the business, and their youngest son James who is currently the manager of the Weston branch, along with their competent and knowledgeable staff, continue to serve both the novice and experienced player alike.

Over forty years have elapsed since Brian's first promotion at the Red Lion Hotel in Somerton but his resolve remains steadfast. There have been many pitfalls – Brian maintains that he fell into most of them – but from humble beginnings his 'Walk on the Westside' has created a company whose name is synonymous with quality and courtesy.

Westside Music at Bridge Street, Taunton.

Introduction

Do you remember Blackjacks, Owbridge's cough medicine – and the dessert spoonful of malt that the lady at the clinic used to force-feed you every week? What about Uncle Mac, the Ovaltinies, and Dick Tracey? Did you live in the South Somerset area during the fifties and sixties? Did you enjoy popular music in your youth?

If you can answer yes to any of the foregoing questions, I venture to suggest that not only will you have heard of many of the bands featured in this book, you will also have happily bopped the night away to their music.

The groups had their origins in Taunton, Wellington, Chard, Street, Ilminster, Somerton, Yeovil and Minehead, and comprised young men and women who shared a common interest, the love of music. As infants and through their formative years, they would have heard only dance bands and orchestras on the wireless at home, and the compulsory music lessons at school normally involved little more than the communal rendition of songs such as 'London's Burning', and 'Drink To Me Only'. Songs such as these were designed to be sung as 'rounds' and were, quite frankly, as dull as ditchwater. The elderly mother of a keyboard player from the Yeovil area, whom I have come to regard as a great friend, reliably informs me that her son used to hold his breath for long periods during a music lesson at school. This would induce a reddening of the face, a throbbing in the temples and an unprecedented coughing-fit, whereupon his teacher would banish him from the room with the instruction not to return until he had taken in some fresh air and felt better.

The classes were co-educational and many of the pupils, both male and female, lent their voices to the lesson, blissfully unaware that they were tone deaf and incapable of holding a tune even if it were placed in a bucket. Such was the cacophony raised by a primary school class in Wellington whilst singing 'Drink To Me Only', that the music teacher was prompted to visit the Conservative Club at lunchtime to calm his nerves.

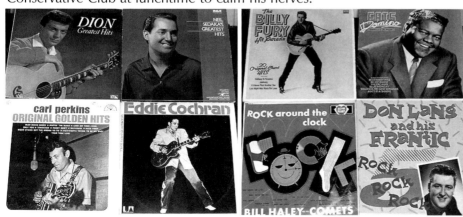

Pupils perceived by the teacher to possess an obvious musical talent were given the opportunity to join the school's recorder band. Please don't misunderstand me, a recorder in the hands of a genius like James Galway can be very soothing, but in the clutches of a rank amateur (whose father just happens to sit on the board of school governors), the instrument has the appeal of a pneumatic drill.

The advent of skiffle, probably the single most influential happening in the history of British pop music, coincided with the commencement of secondary education for the would-be musicians of Somerset. This exciting new genre could for the most part be played using DIY instruments – an inverted tea chest with a broom handle and string proved an inexpensive alternative to a double bass, and a washboard, together with a couple of metal thimbles borrowed from Grandma's sewing box, clearly augmented the rhythm section. A round-hole Spanish guitar could at this time be purchased for a few shillings, and three chords were normally sufficient to accompany the vocals.

Doubtless the skiffle revolution came as a culture shock to many parents. Hitherto accustomed to the sound of their offspring at his or her daily violin practice, struggling to make sense of Debussy's 'Clair de Lune', mums and dads recoiled in horror as their son or daughter, together with a small army of friends, belted out songs such as 'Freight Train', and 'The Grand Coulee Dam'.

The partially-deaf grandmother of a young 'skiffler' from Wellington who, on the death of her husband had moved in with her in-laws, was the envy of her son and daughter in-law. The old lady watched and listened with interest as her grandson strummed his guitar and bellowed out a song called 'Cumberland Gap'. When the boy had finished the song his grandmother politely applauded and said, 'You can see it from the top of the monument you know.'

Totally confused, the boy asked, 'See what, Grandma?'

'Sidmouth Gap,' the lady replied. 'It's in Devon. I went there once with your Grandfather.'

With the benefit of hindsight, parents are generally in accord that worse was to come! By the mid-to-late fifties, rock and roll had begun to eclipse both big band music and skiffle. It was drastically changing the field of popular music, and the kids loved it! Where skiffle had been melodious, rock and roll was manic. The music had drive and a rawness that was almost tangible.

Teenaged musicians in Somerset, as elsewhere all over the country, stepped up a gear. Washboard players became drummers, and tea chest bassists bought six-string guitars – detuned to give a lower-pitched sound. Guitarists who until recently had been conversant with only three or four chords bought 'Teach Yourself' books such as Bert Weedon's excellent *Play in a Day*, and became familiar with twelve-bar and four-chord sequences. Pickups were added to acoustic guitars and old valve radios and reel-to-reel tape recorders were utilised as amplifiers until such times when a 'real' instrument and amplifier could be acquired.

In most cases the acquisition of a 'brand-name' guitar and amplifier, drum kit, keyboard or saxophone etc. hinged on the willingness of the paternal parent to append his name to a hire-purchase form. This situation was rarely negated, even when the youth commenced full-time employment. As an example: an apprentice's net weekly income at this time would have been approximately £4. A secondhand Hofner solid-bodied guitar could be purchased for about £30. Add to this figure a protective hard-shell case, a guitar strap and a lead, and the resulting figure represents over two months' wages. Assuming that a present-day unmarried apprentice finds himself on the minimum wage of £4.50 an hour, his net weekly wage will be in the order of £130 per week, based on a forty-hour week. These days, 'starter packages' are readily available from any reputable music shop and comprise a beautifully-finished solid-bodied guitar, a strap and a lead, an electric tuner, a gig bag and an amplifier – for under £200.

Notwithstanding the above, a musician inevitably secured the instrument of his dreams, with or without dad's signature.

Thanks to the foresight and determination of men like Brian Mapstone, village halls throughout Somerset that had previously hosted nothing more raucous than a whist- or beetle-drive, reverberated to the sound of rock and roll. As the crowds got bigger so larger venues were booked to accommodate them: the Corn Exchange in Chard, the Town Halls in Street and Bridgwater, the County Ballroom in Taunton, and of course Glastonbury Town Hall, to mention but a few. Cinemas too were regularly commandeered to showcase local talent by way of 'beat competitions'.

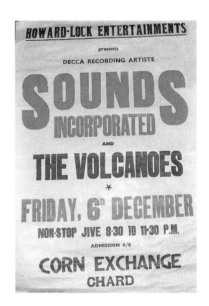

The biographies contained in this book tell of countless hours of rehearsal by young men and women in search of perfection – which brought several bands to the very brink of national acclaim. Without exception, all of the featured outfits supported professional touring acts that were currently enjoying, or were to soon enjoy, chart success. These included Gene Vincent, P.P. Arnold, Procol Harum, The Tremeloes, The Troggs, The Searchers, The Hollies, and in later years the Bay City Rollers – the list is endless.

One wonders where some of the bands from Somerset would be today had they originated in the South Eastern corner of the country rather than the Westcountry. Even Bristol, home to many very fine rock and roll outfits, appeared to be habitually overlooked by record producers and talent scouts. Stumpy of course, and Justin's Timepiece, both cut discs that were extremely commercial, both records receiving valuable air play and both selling in huge quantities, but once again the Westcountry syndrome ensured that neither waxing made it into the charts.

My good friend Dave 'Dan'l' Wood and I have travelled thousands of miles together during the research stages of this, my third humble offering. We have been overwhelmed by the hospitality shown to us, and are privileged to call the musicians of Somerset, friends. We are delighted that Volumes One and Two of *Oh No! It's Local Rock and Roll… but I like it* – which trace the roots of rock and roll, in Mid and East Devon respectively, appear to have sparked a mini rock revival in both of these areas.

In conversation with Dan'l at a recent Son-Set reunion gig, vocalist Chris Abrahams commented upon the fact that he had thoroughly enjoyed meeting all the musicians at the Devon Cliffs Holiday Park in Exmouth who had gathered to assist in the official launch of the last book. 'It was just like one big family,' he said.

With the publication of this book the family grows ever larger. Research into the bands from the Torbay, Plymouth and North Devon areas has already commenced, and a further book covering the rock and rollers of Cornwall is planned. God and my publisher (which to an author amounts to much the same person) willing, the aforementioned books will be produced prior to my retirement in a residential home for the terminally upbeat.

Barry Sowden
Tiverton
2004

The Groups

PART ONE

The Avalon's at Spaxton. l–r: Les Blackmore, John McGinn, Clive Terrill, Barry Denman.

The Avalons

Myth has it that Glastonbury sits upon the former Isle of Avalon in the Somerset marshes, and one could be forgiven for mistakenly assuming that the band originated there. The outfit was in fact based in Taunton, and took its name from a popular American singer who made several incursions into the lower reaches of the British Hit Parade ('Charts'), called Frankie Avalon.

From the Priorswood area, fifteen-year-old John McGinn first met Barry Denman at the Emlyn Rees Music shop in the High Street where Barry worked as a sales assistant. Both novice guitarists, the two young men often met at Barry's home, playing skiffle and the odd Ventures instrumental, and practising in his father's garage, a small construction built specifically to house a motorcycle and side-car.

Left: John McGinn. Right: Barry Denman.

John's father, also called John but known to all as Jock, sometimes visited the Bell Inn at Creech St Michael with friends. The Bell, a homely hostelry, occasionally provided live entertainment for its patrons on Saturday evenings in the form of a little duo comprising drummer Les Blackmore and a local man who played the banjo. Jock became friendly with the musical twosome and mentioned that his son John and his mate played the guitar. Les Blackmore who, unlike his banjo-strumming colleague, wanted to play music of a more modern genre, was eventually persuaded by Jock to team up with his son and Barry Denman.

A variety show organised by Emlyn Rees Music and held in the village hall at Spaxton, near Taunton, provided the trio with the opportunity to gauge the reaction of a live audience as to their musical ability. The applause that followed each of the five instrumental numbers played was polite, though not earth shattering, and gave the boys much encouragement. Nevertheless, it was patently obvious to John and Barry that a bass guitarist was needed if the group was to produce a sound similar to that of their two favourite groups, The Shadows and The Ventures. Additionally, Barry Denman thought that a vocalist should be found. 'Instrumentals are great to play and good for dancing,' he said, 'but I wouldn't want to play them all night!' Les Blackmore was fully in agreement with both sentiments and added that if the band was going to 'employ' a bass player, both John and Barry would have to buy electric guitars and amplifiers.

It was fortunate that Barry Denman recruited singer Clive Terrill before a bassist was found, as it gave John McGinn time to build an electric guitar. Shortly after the Spaxton concert John, who had left school some three weeks earlier, was indentured as an apprentice pattern maker with a company called Easton & Johnson, a division of the Reed & Smith Paper

John McGinn with his Easton & Johnson 'Special'.

group, at their works in Albermarle Road. With access to machine and hand tooling, the assent of his foreman and the help of a couple of workmates, John made himself a six-string solid-bodied electric guitar during his coffee and lunch breaks.

The finished instrument was virtually unplayable. John knew nothing of fret spacing and even less about the twelfth-fret principle. Desperate to know why his creation did not function as it should, John consulted a gentleman called Chris Legg. The father of Sabres bass guitarist Dave Legg, Chris set up the guitar as best he could. 'At least,' Chris said, 'I've been able to tune it now. Whether it stays that way is a very different matter!' Just one month later, the fretting and tuning problems became somewhat academic…

Cycling over to Barry Denman's house for the usual weekly practice with the guitar slung inverted across his back, John was suddenly hurled sideways from his bike. The guitar had slipped and the machine-head had become enmeshed in the spokes of the rear wheel. Thankfully John suffered no physical damage. The same could not be said for the guitar or the bicycle. The machine head looked as though it had been attacked by a colony of beavers and the neck had been damaged beyond repair. The back wheel of the bike was twisted and would without doubt need replacing. John returned to his house and, pausing only to tell his mother that he'd fallen off his bike and that he was unhurt, collected his Spanish guitar and walked to Lansdown Road. A new neck, complete with machine head, was produced at Easton & Johnson accompanied by much micky-taking from his colleagues.

When Mike Green, a cub reporter with the *Somerset County Gazette* newspaper, joined The Avalons as the bass guitarist, Barry Denman's parents insisted that the band find a new practice venue. Not of course that they had anything against Mike whom they both thought a very sensible and likeable young man. No, it was the rhythmic and low-pitched throbbing of his bass that seemed to vibrate through the walls of the garage into their living room, and which had Mr and Mrs D. reaching for the aspirin.

Spot the new boys! l–r: John McGinn, Keith Boobyer, Dave Stratford, Barry Denman, Brian Blackmore.

In deference to Barry's parents, rehearsals were subsequently held in a barn at Nerrell's Farm, between Priorswood and Creech St Michael. John's 'Easton & Johnson Special' sounded surprisingly good when connected to an old valve radio set. He had volume to spare, although not much, and it was clearly audible above Mike and Barry's guitars, Les Blackmore's kit and Clive's voice.

The Avalons certainly sounded good at the youth clubs in Chard and Ilminster. The membership loved their music, and they received return bookings from both organisations. Following the dance at Ilminster youth club, however, during the latter half of which he thought he saw a wisp of smoke emanating from the vents at the rear of the radio, John purchased a Vox AC15 amplifier.

Mike Green, who had obviously found his vocation as a 'newshound', left the band after six months, his position being filled by local boy Bernard 'Chubby' Oaten. Chubby had been recommended to Barry Denman by highly-respected Taunton bass guitarist Dave Stratford, a regular visitor to Emlyn Rees Music.

The musicians of South Somerset were delighted when Taunton danceband-leader Sid Roberts bought a franchise from Minns Music and opened a shop in the High Street. Sid was very well-respected locally, as was his wife who ran a dancing class at the hall in the Galmington area of the town. Among Sid's first customers were The Avalons – or at least the guitar-playing members of The Avalons, namely John, Barry Denman and Chubby. All three guitarists had raised sufficient finance to place a deposit on the guitar of their choice – provided that the instrument selected was within the parameters of their budget, and all three selected British-made Burns guitars.

Sid Roberts produced three hire-purchase agreements and asked the boys to fill in their name and current address. Eager to get his guitar home John perused his form quickly. At the foot of the second page John noticed a clause which clearly stated that the signatory to the agreement must be aged twenty-one or over. He sighed audibly. 'Problem?' asked Dave Stratford who had been browsing the array of bass guitars. John pointed to the clause and explained his predicament.

'The repayments are no big deal. We've got bookings coming in left right and centre, but father will never stand guarantor, he doesn't believe in hire-purchase.'

'I presume Barry and Chubby are in the same boat then,' said Dave.

'Yeah, I guess so,' replied John.

'Well,' said Dave, 'I've known Sid for a long time – let's see what we can do.'

John, Barry and Chubby left Minns Music with new guitars and new Vox amplifiers – Dave Stratford having agreed to guarantee the payments from all three musicians.

The new equipment seemed to inject fervour into the band that had not previously existed. Clive Terrill's cover versions of his idol Gene Vincent's 'Be Bop-A-Lula', 'Bluejean Bop' and 'Git It' were delivered with passion, and Les Blackmore for the first time in his life discovered that the drumsticks he was currently using were simply not heavy enough.

The outfit's popularity increased apace and, as always, Murphy's law struck. 'Murphy's law?' You know the one. 'If something possibly can go wrong, it will!' Les Blackmore decided that he could not cope with the volume of work that was being offered to the band, and he was followed out of the group by vocalist Clive Terrill – presumably for the same reason. Colin Hayes acted as a stopgap for Les Blackmore prior to Keith Boobyer becoming the band's permanent sticksman, and talented, often underrated, vocalist Brian Blackmore, accepted an offer from Dave Stratford on the band's behalf, to become The Avalons' new front man.

The period that followed was, in the opinion of founder-members John and Barry, The Avalons' most successful. Keith Boobyer was proving a godsend. He had taken the band by the scruff of the neck as it were, adopted the position of stage leader, provided harmony vocal backing, and given the band presence. For more than three years The Avalons vied with The Sabres and The Mustangs for the title of top local band, and was often voted into first place ahead of their rivals. Still a semi-professional outfit, such was the demand for the band's services that Jock McGinn was appointed as manager to deal with all enquiries and confirmations. When the band appeared at the Riverside Rooms – now Deller's Café in Taunton – the police were called to assist with 'crowd control'. The queue stretched for almost one hundred metres.

At the Winter Gardens Pavilion in Weston-super-Mare, The Avalons won their heat in the 'Westcountry Beat Competition' in the face of some stiff competition from the likes of the locally-based Ivies, and Dulverton's Stringbeats.

In the course of his work as a civil servant, Jock McGinn was sent to Cyprus. Prior to his departure, being fully aware of The Avalons' popularity and potential, Jock spoke to Les Laverock, the manager of both the Odeon Cinema and The Sabres, and asked him if he would kindly 'keep an eye on things' in his absence. A shrewd businessman, Les visualised the benefits of managing two of the top three local outfits, and agreed to 'mind the store' pending Jock's return.

The Laverock-staged Av-Sab shows – featuring The Avalons and The Sabres – were a dance aficionado's dream. The 'split-break' functions were hugely successful, each of the bands 'strutting their stuff' in an effort to achieve 'top dog status'. The intense rivalry between the two groups served only to improve both individual and collective performances. Generally speaking there was an equal number of fans from both camps present, so neither band could categorically claim to have 'won the battle'. On one particularly busy weekend, The Avalons performed at the Territorial Hall in Bishops Hull on the Friday evening, took part in a talent competition at the Winter Gardens in Weston-super-Mare on the Saturday afternoon, and played at Ile Hale in Ilminster on the Saturday evening. Sunday afternoon found the band at the Odeon Cinema in company with The Sabres, and the weekend was rounded off with an appearance at the Khyber Club.

The morning of 26 December 1963 saw a procession of assorted vehicles – led by John McGinn in 'Manfred', his 1937 Ford Eight motor car – so named because the numbers 543 on the registration plate reminded him of the Manfred Mann chart-topper 5,4,3,2,1 – leave Taunton en route to Ross-on-Wye in Herefordshire where The Avalons were to entertain the members of a large social club at their annual Christmas party. The weather had not been kind, a mixture of rain, sleet and snow had made the roads treacherous, and the boys were conscious of the need to take extra care. The convoy reached Ross-on-Wye at three o'clock, and located the social club without difficulty, thanks to directions supplied by an on-duty, unhappy policeman.

With the exception of a large black Morris Commercial van, the car park adjoining the club was deserted. Brian Blackmore knocked firmly on the main entrance door while Keith Boobyer and John strolled around to the rear of the building. They reappeared within minutes to report that there was no sign of life anywhere.

Manfred and friends.

'I wonder who owns that old van?' said John.

'Probably some bloke who had a few too many at lunchtime and decided to leg-it home,' replied Brian Blackmore. 'Why don't we go into the town, get something to eat, and come back later, I'm starving!'

'Come to think of it,' said Barry Denman, 'I'm a bit peckish myself, let's go.'

On their return, the boys were pleased to note that the premises were fully illuminated and that there were two cars parked neatly alongside the front

The Avalons at the Odeon Cinema in Corporation Street, Taunton.

wall. Parking their vehicles almost as tidily, The Avalons prepared to unload their equipment.

'I don't think we ought to unload the gear just yet,' said Dave Stratford pointing to the old Morris van that they had seen earlier – which was now parked with its rear doors gaping in front of a pair of doors leading into the club. 'Looks like we've got a support act with us – perhaps we can use the same PA, that'll save us humping ours in.'

'Either that, or somebody's cocked-up and double-booked,' said Keith.

To their dismay, Keith's pessimism was well founded. There had apparently been a mid-year change of secretary at the club – and the former had failed to inform the new incumbent that he had secured entertainment for the Boxing Day party.

By the time that the mix up was finally sorted out, the owners of the Morris van had begun their sound check. The Avalons, having been engaged by the new secretary and therefore 'second favourites' to supply the evening's entertainment, decided to go back to the Victoria Rooms in Bristol on a busman's holiday and watch which ever outfit happened to be appearing that night. John McGinn recalls the Ross-on-Wye fiasco as being the only time that The Avalons were ever double-booked, in the six-plus years that he was with them.

By 1964, Jock McGinn was becoming accustomed to being despatched, often with as little as twenty-four hours notice, to the far-flung corners of the globe, and conceded that he could no longer discharge his duties as manager of The Avalons. For the next eighteen months the boys collectively dealt with the administrative side of the group, and subsequently discovered how lucky they had been to have this task undertaken by Jock and or Les Laverock.

Drummer Keith Boobyer 'depping' with the Reg Gray Dance Band: l–r: Keith, Derek Bardon, Ken Ford, Reg Gray.

The Avalons went through a complete renaissance at the end of 1965. Keith Boobyer stepped back in time by returning to the dance-band scene – firstly with the Colin Day Orchestra, Colin having been the accompanying pianist for legendary singer Donald Peers – and later with the Raymond Kaye Orchestra. The vacancy created by Keith's departure was filled by rhythm guitarist Barry Denman who for some time had fancied playing the drums, and vocalist Rod Hake stepped up to the microphone as front man following Brian Blackmore's departure.

John McGinn, who privately thought that The Avalons had peaked and were presently on the downhill path, remained with the outfit until the middle of 1966, when he left the band to team up once more with Brian Blackmore in a duo called 'Penny Halfpenny'.

In the years that followed, The Avalons' line-up changed many times: Peter Milner, Duncan Yandle, Terry Jarvis, and Dave 'Skinny' Anderson – a superb guitarist in his own right – being just four of the many musicians who featured. When The Avalons finally disbanded, long-serving bass guitarist Dave Stratford, just as Keith Boobyer had done previously, returned to his roots in the traditional dance-band arena. He remains to this day the consummate professional and is a member of the Denny Blackmore Band.

The Beatmakers latterly known as Penny Arcade

Of Polish extraction, but born in Llangollen, North Wales, Witold (pronounced 'Vee-told'), Budzynsky and his brother Wieslaw (pronounced 'Vees-lav'), moved, via Sherborne, to Yeovil with their parents in 1960. Witold loved to listen to music from the late fifties, and especially enjoyed rock and roll. His brother possessed a large collection of records, both 78 and 45rpm, and Witold became a master of the 'air-guitar' using an old tennis racket.

Enrolled as a student at the Technical College in Yeovil some years later, ostensibly to prepare for a proposed career as an electrician, Bud (as his fellow students called him), immediately contacted the senior tutor in the woodworking department, and requested his permission to build a guitar during the lunch hours and between lectures.

Steve Tucker getting to grips with six strings.

The guitar when built was at least playable, and needed only a coat of paint to complete the project. Bud found a paintbrush and an old can of paint in his father's shed – the label had long since gone and oxidisation had beset the lid, but he decided that the contents might be useable and carried the can to the kitchen. Covering the polished top of the kitchen table with sheets of newspaper, he placed the can on the table and carefully prised off the lid with the blunt edge of a bread knife. Peering into the can he noted that the film that had formed on top of the paint was red, a very bright red! Bud thought the colour reminiscent of a Post Office pillar-box and eminently suitable for the handcrafted instrument. Taking a fish knife from the drawer he made an incision in the protective skin covering the paint, and was delighted to note that the paint appeared to have retained its liquidity. Removing and discarding the film entirely, Bud laid the guitar on the table, took paintbrush in hand and applied the first strokes. Some thirty minutes later he regarded his handiwork and came to the conclusion that another coat was definitely needed – the new wood had accepted the paint like a sponge. He had, he reasoned, about an hour to wait before applying the next coat, and resolved to make full use of the time by cycling into town to buy a set of strings. Loosely fitting the lid to the can of paint, Bud laid the brush aside and left the house...

He returned with the strings in his pocket and a smile on his face. He had bumped into Steve Tucker, a friend from the Technical College, in the music shop and Steve had promised to come over that afternoon with his bass guitar, also home-made, for a practice session. Back in the kitchen Bud tentatively applied the tip of his index finger to the back of the guitar, noted with approval that the paint was perfectly dry, and found himself wondering what the instrument looked like when 'worn in the playing position'.

Unable to resist, he found some string, looped it around the top and bottom of the guitar and slung the instrument over his shoulder. It was then that disaster struck! The loop slipped off the strap-locating button at the bottom of the guitar, and the instrument bounced off the kitchen table on to the floor, his agile but futile lunge to save the guitar serving only to knock the can of paint over. With commendable speed Bud righted the can, stepping on the neck of his guitar as he did so with a shattering crunch. From a kneeling position, surrounded by cleaning rags, sundry proprietary cleaning agents and a bucket, Bud relayed the details of the accident to his mother on her return from the shops, and apologised for the overwhelming smell of turpentine in the kitchen and upon his clothes.

Two hours had elapsed by the time that the kitchen table and floor were restored to their former pristine condition. Steve Tucker had called as arranged and, having ascertained the reason for his friend's genuflection, departed with a snigger promising to call back later. Bud's brother, Wieslaw, had been compelled to withdraw to the sitting-room to drink his coffee, and was having great difficulty in suppressing his laughter.

In all honesty, Bud was torn between laughing and crying, the incident would not have been out of place in a stage farce. He glanced ruefully at the splintered neck of the guitar and wondered momentarily whether it could be glued, or screwed, back into its original and rightful position. Closer inspection confirmed that was definitely not the case. The instrument was beyond repair!

The Rayngers at the Gang Show. l–r: Steve Tucker, Dave Allen, John Pearce, Witold 'Bud' Budzynsky.

'So what are you going to do then mate?' asked Steve Tucker later that

afternoon. 'Save up and buy a proper one, or make another at college?'

'I haven't given it much thought yet,' replied Bud, 'but I've got no money at the moment, and little likelihood of getting any in the near future, so I suppose it's back to the woodwork room at lunchtimes for me.'

At the start of the following week Wieslaw, who had overheard the conversation and realising just how upset Bud really was, bought a guitar together with a 'Teach Yourself' book, and presented it to his younger brother. Overjoyed, Bud immediately set about learning to play. He proved to have natural ability and was soon playing chords and single note solos with equal dexterity. He and Steve Tucker practised regularly at Steve's home, and the enjoyment derived from these musical soirées was evident.

The St Michael's & All Angels 2nd Yeovil Scout Troop, to which Steve had belonged for some years, gave the boys the opportunity to display their musical expertise. In the winter of 1963 as part of their ongoing crusade to raise sufficient finances to fund the building of a new scout hut, the scout leaders, together with several interested parents, proposed that the troop stage a 'Gang Show'. Steve volunteered his and Bud's services, enlisting the aid of fellow scouts John Pearce and Dave Allen, and formed a band they called The Rayngers. With Steve and Bud playing acoustic guitars, John Pearce heading the vocal department and Dave Allen using a snare drum loaned to him by Steve Tucker, the lads rehearsed a ten-minute set, which they performed some three weeks later to a capacity crowd at St Michael's Hall in Yeovil. Steve recalls that they were extremely nervous at the outset, but that the warmth of the welcome, and the hearty applause that followed each of their numbers, stimulated the adrenaline and did their confidence a power of good.

Although John Pearce and Dave Allen had neither the time nor the desire to repeat the performance, Steve and Bud could not wait to relive the experience and the show was the main topic of conversation for several days. News of the show quickly spread and they were soon joined by two friends Ian Lucas and Don Morgan. Ian and Don had played guitar and drums respectively for some time, owned their own equipment and fitted the criteria perfectly.

The band, now called The Beatmakers, accepted a booking at Stoford near Yeovil with but one qualm, transport. None of the lads was old enough to drive, and the thought of walking the three miles to Stoford with armsful of gear was a daunting prospect. Bud's elder brother, Wieslaw, the proprietor of his own aerial erecting business, quickly solved this problem by offering to take the boys and their equipment to the gig in his Bedford Dormobile van. At the little hall in Stoford, having assisted with the unloading and setting-up of the kit, Wieslaw listened as the boys warmed up with an instrumental and was pleasantly surprised. These boys, he thought, are really quite good! He had often thought that it would be fun to sing with a band and was sure that he possessed enough flair to become a front man. Jumping on to the little wooden stage he grabbed the microphone from its stand and said, 'Let's do it.'

Dale Fender and The Beatmakers. l–r: Steve Tucker, Don Morgan, Witold 'Bud' Budzynsky, Ian Lucas. Seated: Wieslaw Budzynsky (Dale Fender).

Wieslaw's enthusiasm more than compensated for his lack of experience and he became The Beatmakers' vocalist from that evening on. Throwing himself into weekly rehearsals, he adopted the stage name Dale Fender – Dale being the name of one of his favourite television and film actors Dale Robertson of 'Wells Fargo' fame, and Fender, the manufacturer of his brand-new recently purchased amplifier.

During the next eighteen months The Beatmakers slowly and methodically amassed a repertoire worthy of a professional outfit. Supporters of the band often commented on the fact that the boys always seemed to be able to play all the current hits almost as soon as the records hit the shops. They were of course not to know that Steve Tucker had devised a most ingenious method of acquiring both music and lyrics.

Piracy at Bowler & Goddards.

Steve and Bud frequently called at a music shop in Yeovil called Bowler & Goddards. Normally on a Saturday morning, the visits were ostensibly designed to preview, and perhaps purchase, the latest record releases. Given a lightweight, battery-driven, reel-to-reel tape recorder with a similarly compact condenser microphone as a Christmas present, Steve would stroll up to the counter and nonchalantly ask the ever-obliging shop assistant if he could listen to a newly released vinyl single – the chosen record being a song or instrumental that The Beatmakers particularly wanted to learn. The assistant would invariably smile and direct Steve to a booth, not unlike a modern open-plan telephone kiosk, return to his or her position behind the counter, select the appropriate disc from stock and play it on a turntable that was connected by wires to the sound booth. This gave Steve ample time to place the tape recorder on a handily-sited shelf, press the record button and 'pirate' the music. With Bud acting as a screen by standing at his shoulder,

Steve was never caught in the act. When the record had finished, Steve merely popped the microphone in his pocket, closed the lid of the recorder, and after thanking the assistant for his or her trouble, left the shop saying, 'I'm not sure about the record, I'll think about it.'

With each new engagement came new support and appreciation of their rapidly improving act. Regularly featured in the media, Dale Fender and The Beatmakers began to attract the attention of agents from Dorset, Avon, Hampshire and Wiltshire, which enhanced an already healthy diary.

On one particularly busy and memorable weekend in the early part of 1965, Dale and the boys embarked upon a micro-mini tour. The lads left Yeovil on the Friday afternoon, Bud and Steve having just completed that day's tutorials at college, en route to the Stonehenge Inn at Amesbury in Wiltshire where they were to provide the entertainment that evening. The Dormobile had been loaded with a little more care than usual due to some additional luggage – Steve Tucker's two-man tent, a camping stove and utensils, blankets and pillows, and not forgetting essential survival rations like cans of beer, cigarettes and chocolate. Don Morgan's drums had been consigned to the roof and, at Dale's insistence, personally lashed down by the drummer, reasoning that if any of the kit fell off it would be entirely his own fault.

Local bookings are best! The Beatmakers at Stoford Village Hall.

The journey to Amesbury was uneventful, although on their arrival rhythm guitarist Ian Lucas, Don's co-passenger in the rear of the van grumbled that he was suffering with cramp, and laughingly enquired as to how the rest of the band expected him to stand up all night when he could hardly walk! Ian and the boys did in fact play extremely well and enjoyed a thoroughly pleasant evening. The patrons of the cosy olde-world Stonehenge Inn proved to be appreciative of the band's efforts, and the venue became one to which The Beatmakers returned on many occasions.

The outside temperature had dropped considerably by the time the boys had packed up, and they were delighted to accept the landlord's offer of a sandwich and a hot toddy prior to leaving. Dale had previously selected a quiet spot on Salisbury Plain in which to park, or in Steve Tucker's case, pitch overnight. Steve's years in the scouts standing him in fine stead, he had his tent erected within ten minutes and, having retrieved his sleeping bag, pillow and blankets from the van, wished the rest of the boys a very good night. Climbing into his sleeping bag he was asleep within minutes. In the Dormobile and for varying reasons, Dale, Bud, Ian and Don slept fitfully.

A light sleeper, Steve awoke to a sound he describes as being a cross between a chainsaw and a tractor. Climbing out of his sleeping bag, he unzipped the tent flap and rubbed his eyes in disbelief. A military tank, since identified as a Centurion, was rumbling across the plain in his general direction. Quickly vacating the tent, Steve rushed to the van and woke the others. The noise was deafening as the vehicle passed. Bud glanced at his watch. 'Aw heck,' he groaned, 'it's only six o'clock – we didn't get to bed until nearly three!'

Needless to say, Dale and The Beatmakers reached Andover, their next and final port of call mid-morning on Saturday, and following a trencherman's breakfast at a little café, wandered rather aimlessly around the town taking in a couple of well-stocked music shops. Pointing to a large poster which announced that top American vocal harmony group, The Byrds, were appearing in Andover that evening, Bud grinned and said to his colleagues, 'They'll only do a couple of forty-minute spots, so they'll probably come and watch us afterwards.'

Dale and the boys located the venue for their gig, an imposing building called the Fiesta Hall, without difficulty, and they were set up and ready to rock by seven o'clock. Despite the fact that, apart from themselves and the gentleman who had let them into the building, the room was devoid of life, they took the stage at eight o'clock and played their first number.

The situation changed slightly at about 10.15pm when two attractive young ladies entered the hall. Unfortunately, their entry coincided with the band taking a break which, although they had largely treated the occasion as a practice session, they felt they richly deserved. Dale made a beeline for the two girls and asked, 'Where is everybody?'

The taller of the two girls replied, 'I think most people have gone to see The Byrds, they're supposed to be brilliant.' As if to emphasise the point, her friend quickly added, 'We would have gone too, but we couldn't get tickets!'

The boys resumed at 10.30pm and played through until 11.45pm – the time scheduled for the evening to end. Audience-wise it had doubtless been the quietest night ever, but as Bud philosophically remarked later, the band had managed to learn two new numbers.

In the winter of 1965, the boys were offered the chance to showcase their talents in Europe, in Germany to be precise, where they would entertain military and civilian men and women serving with the United States Air Force. Additionally, the twelve-month tour was to take in several clubs situated in the south of the country. Acceptance of the contract meant of course that the boys would have to become professional musicians and forsake their current employment. Dale, Bud, Ian and Don considered the opportunity too good to miss and, where applicable, gave notice of their intention to quit their present jobs. It must be said that Mr and Mrs Budzynsky senior were mortified when they were informed by their youngest son that he would not be completing his apprenticeship as an electrician, and were only partially mollified by the fact that their eldest son would be on hand to keep a fraternal eye on him.

Waiting for an audience at the Fiesta Hall, Amesbury.

Apprenticed with the GPO (General Post Office), Steve Tucker decided against the professional option and was replaced by John Wilmington. Formerly the bass guitarist with The Jaguars, another very popular Yeovil outfit, John had known Dale and the boys for many years and was happy in their company. There was an air of expectancy in the little two-toned Dormobile as the boys set off on the outward leg of the journey. They were fully aware that they had been recommended to Gisella Gunther, the entertainment agent from Germany to whom they were now contracted, by some friends and fellow musicians from Poole in Dorset, and were determined to repay the faith that had been placed in them. And for nine months they did just that. Each performance was treated as if it was by royal command, and the Americans loved every minute.

Sadly, the tour ended prematurely. In the midst of a show in September 1966, bass guitarist John Wilmington was asked to go to the base commander's office to take an urgent telephone call. The call from the British Consulate informed John that his father Robert, or Bob as he was more affectionately known, had been suddenly and quite unexpectedly taken ill and tragically died. John returned home immediately, and the remaining tour dates were cancelled.

Another piece of bad luck – though by comparison to the news that John had received the matter was a trifling if annoying affair – awaited The Beatmakers when they reached the German–French border. Whilst on tour, a couple of the boys had treated themselves to some new gear, Bud for example had purchased his dream guitar, a brand-spanking-new Gibson semi-acoustic. Several factors had made this possible. Instruments were generally subject to less import duty in Germany, and at this time, sterling was particularly healthy. The main reason, however, was the fact that the Americans were 'picking up the tab' for all of the band's accommodation and meals.

Lots of people enjoy a good haggle and the Budzynsky lads were no different to anyone else. If Bud could obtain a discount of fifty or a hundred pounds by waving a handful of pound notes in the face of a German music shop proprietor rather than setting up a finance deal, he would. Further, if he could avoid local taxes by paying in cash, he was not that bothered about a receipt. Consequently, when asked to provide proof of ownership for some pieces of equipment which, even to the uninitiated were obviously straight out of the showroom, Dale and Bud were unable to oblige the gentlemen from the German equivalent of HM Customs and Excise.

THE HIGH POST HOTEL
PRESENTS
in THE STARLIGHT ROOM,
on FRIDAY, 19th APRIL 1974
THE
BARRON KNIGHTS
SUPPORTED BY
PENNY ARCADE
9-T   ADMISSION £2.00

Back in Yeovil, the disillusioned members of The Beatmakers turned their backs on a professional career in music and acquired for themselves what the majority of parents call real jobs. The band underwent two or three changes of name before finally adopting one that had been suggested by Wieslaw, Penny Arcade. Ex-Beatmaker Steve Tucker returned in the capacity of road manager and electrician, and the band veered towards cabaret rather than rock and roll. Old friendships with agencies like Ace Music in Salisbury, Howard T. Lock Entertainment, and Frank Huddy's Double 'H' were renewed, and the Budzynsky brothers once again took the band to the very top of the local scene.

There have been many changes of personnel between 1966 and the present day: superb musicians such as guitarists Mike Lapthorne, and Phil Kelly, currently with Bruce Welch's Moonlight Shadows; drummers Bob Tucker, and Adrian Lewis formerly with a band from Shepton Mallet called Patsy and

The Pretenders, keyboard maestro Clive Lever, and alto saxophonist Tony Watson have all taken the stage as members of Penny Arcade. Now under the leadership of Witold (Bud) Budzynsky, Penny Arcade is unquestionably Yeovil's premier cabaret outfit. Bud's three-octave-range voice, and the showmanship and experience that he has gained from years in the music business, make the band versatile in the extreme.

Penny Arcade. l–r: Dale Fender, Adrian Lewis, Clive Lever, Tony Edwards, Bud Budzynsky.

The Cortinas

also known as Steve and the Bandits, and the Tornadoes

Eight-year-old Steve Stimpson sat on his bed and watched the sun set slowly over the Taj Mahal. He picked up the ukulele that his brother Ernest (whom the family called Bill), had given him all those years ago, and gently drew his fingertip across the four soft nylon strings. He grimaced as he did so – the top two strings were way out of tune, but he made no effort to correct them. Tearfully the boy placed the little instrument on the top of his bedside-cabinet, lay down and tried to sleep.

He and his mother were to sail to England on the following day. His brother George (whom everyone called Alfie or Stim) was to meet the family at Liverpool in three weeks' time, from where they would travel to a place called Yeovil. His last letter had said that Yeovil was not as big as Agra – but was very nice, and the people were friendly.

Born in Agra, in the state of Uttar Pradesh in India, Steve had recently contracted tuberculosis, in his left leg. The debilitating illness, a bacterial infection which in the majority of cases attacks the respiratory system but can also affect other parts of the body, was diagnosed by the family doctor who gravely informed the boy's parents that the drugs necessary to control the disease were not readily available, and that regular treatment would not be possible.

Nevertheless, the GP stated that he would do everything in his power to contain the problem. Steve's father, himself terminally ill, and fearful that the other members of his family would become infected by the boy's condition, resolved to send the family to England where he hoped his son might be completely cured. Tragically, Steve's father passed away before seeing his family leave their homeland.

Within days of his family's arrival at Alfie's home in Allingham Road, Yeovil, Steve was transported by ambulance to the Royal United Hospital in Bath where he was to receive treatment as both in-patient and out-patient, for a total of three and a half years.

An amiable and conscientious boy, Steve was enrolled as a pupil at Penmill Primary School where with diligence and hard work he was able to surmount the difficulties caused by his enforced absences. He usually walked to and from the school although Alfie would sometimes give him a lift in his car when it was raining, and took pleasure from looking at people's houses and gardens. He considered it to be his duty now that he was a bona-fide citizen of Great Britain, to learn as much as he could about his adopted country. He had noted that during these summer months, people spent many hours in their gardens, planting and hoeing, weeding and sowing. Observing the elderly gentleman in the garden of number 55 Highfield Road expertly wielding a long-handled shovel, Steve looked at his watch, it was nearly twenty past four…

He strolled on, nearing the bottom of Highfield Road, pausing only to retie an errant shoelace. From his crouching position he glanced across the road, which he thought to himself was unusually quiet for that time of the day, and was surprised to see a man of about nineteen or twenty sitting on the front doorstep playing a guitar. Steve crossed to the opposite kerb and stood silently watching – partially obscured by the boundary fence. Captivated by the music, Steve peered around the hedge and he heard himself say, 'That was smashing, you must have been playing the guitar for a long time.'

Christopher Robins, an employee of the Clothier & Giles Leather Company in Adderwell Lane, had indeed been playing the guitar for several years, and was extremely proficient. An amiable man, Chris chatted freely to the nine-year-old who related his life-story within minutes. Over a refreshing glass of orange squash brought to the doorstep by Chris' wife Vera, Steve explained that he had once owned, and could play a ukulele, but that it had been left with his grown-up sister, who had stayed in India with her husband and children.

Deeply moved by the boy's story, Chris offered to teach Steve to play the guitar, and it was a very happy nine-year-old that arrived back at Allingham Road over an hour late. Steve apologised to his very worried mother, and told her all about Chris and Vera, the guitar and the orange squash. 'That's as may be,' said his mother, 'but you know you shouldn't talk to strangers! Your tea is stone cold, and you've still got some packing to do – you do remember that we're moving into our own house the day after tomorrow don't you?' Steve politely replied that Chris wasn't a stranger, he was a guitarist and, after all, he hadn't had to accept the invitation to learn to play the guitar; he was starving and could eat a horse, hot or cold, and no he hadn't forgotten that they were moving to Abbey Road.

L–r: Chris Robins, Steve Stimpson, Cedric 'Sedge' Hardwick.

Upon meeting Chris, Steve's mother's fears were quickly dispelled. Chris had insisted that he came to their home, now in Abbey Road in the Larkhill area, to teach the boy, and that the lessons be on Friday evenings as young Stimpo, his nickname for Steve, did not have to go to school the next day.

Chris Robins became a firm family friend, and proved to be an excellent teacher. Stimpo hung on Chris' every word, absorbed information like a sponge and, moreover, retained it. An above-average player within months rather than years, and much to the amusement of Chris Robins, Stimpo was able to impart his newly acquired knowledge to a friend who lived in Wingate Avenue, by the name of Cedric Hardwick. At their weekly get-together, the boys had a wonderful time. The trio was never given a name, and never performed in public. Chris and Cedric both owned guitars, which

they were more than happy to let their pal play, but the situation was not ideal. Stimpo recollects that he was close to tears when Chris and Cedric offered to 'chip in' toward the cost of an inexpensive acoustic guitar, and actually in tears when he was presented with it.

Roll call at the Teenbeat Club.

Stimpo was almost twelve years old when he commenced his secondary education at Grass Royal Secondary Modern School. He had not seen Chris Robins since the last 'skiffle evening' some three weeks earlier, but remembered Chris telling him that he and Vera were going to be busy for a while redecorating the three bedrooms and the bathroom. Stimpo had thought that very strange – giving up playing the guitar to hang some wallpaper. Most odd! Cedric had not attended the last practice session, and Stimpo made a mental note to ask him if there was something wrong, when he next saw him…

At their next meeting, Cedric apologised to his pal for not letting him know that he would not be at the practice, and explained, 'I was at the Teenbeat

Club, it's great – they've got a proper record player and everything, you ought to come along.'

There are many men and women living in Yeovil today who will remember with affection local man Fred Cottrell. Seeing that there were a large number of boys and girls in his neighbourhood who appeared to have little or nothing to do in their leisure time, Fred founded the Teenbeat Club in a large hall connected to the Vicarage in Park Street. At a peppercorn rent, and with his personal assurance that the members would be well-behaved, Fred simply installed his portable Dansette record player together with a few of his own records, and let the youngsters get on with it.

Accepting Cedric's invitation to accompany him to the club, Stimpo recognised several boys from Grass Royal, and immediately set about making new friends. This task was facilitated by Cedric Hardwick who introduced his friend by saying, 'This is Stimpo, he used to live in a big house in India – but he lives in Abbey Road now, and he's a brilliant guitar player.'

Practising in Fred Cottrell's front room. l–r: Steve Stimpson, Ray Hewitt, Sid Johnston, John Wilmington.

A blushing Steve Stimpson confirmed that he did indeed play the guitar, and in answer to a rhetorical statement by a boy called Sid Johnston who said, 'It must be hard to play,' Steve said that in his opinion, anyone could learn to play if they really wanted to. Sid wanted to, as did John Wilmington. Stimpo taught both boys to play the guitar and these two, Stimpo, and a boy named Ray Hewitt who had always fancied playing the drums, formed the Bandits skiffle group. The group became Steve and the Bandits when 'youth leader' Fred Cottrell, having decided that the four-piece was sufficiently competent to entertain the members, designed and produced a poster which boldly stated that Steve and the Bandits would be appearing 'live at the Teenbeat Club' for the very first time.

The boys were extremely nervous. They had of course often practised at the club, but on those occasions they played in a small anteroom and after the initial interest had faded, had been largely ignored. This was different, this time they were doing it 'for real'.

Their worries were unfounded. The event passed with not the slightest sign of unrest from the club members or their guests. There were two positive highlights during the evening; the first, when the string on John Wilmington's tea chest bass, badly frayed from weeks of rehearsal, suffered a compound fracture, and had to be replaced with a length of green, waxed twine from the vicar's greenhouse, and the second, the addition of a young man called Mike Tozer to the band's line-up. Enthusiastic and personable, Mike had asked if he could sing a couple of songs with the band. The audience had thought he was great, and he was invited to become the band's vocalist that very evening.

Fred Cottrell had watched the young musicians' singing and playing with something approaching admiration. He had been especially impressed with young Stimpo, and only wished that a record company like Decca, Pye or

EMI could hear the lad. Unable to banish the thought from his mind, Fred wrote to all three record companies and was delighted to receive a reply from EMI a few days later. The letter from the public relations department thanked Fred for his communication and confirmed that they would be more than happy to listen to the boy. The letter went on to give the date and time of the audition together with directions to the studio. Stimpo's mother was almost as excited as he was; Fred assured her that he would accompany the boy to the studio, and accept full responsibility for his care and conduct throughout the trip.

In London, with a couple of hours to spare before the audition, Fred asked Stimpo if he would like to do some window-shopping in nearby Shaftesbury Avenue. Readily agreeing, although he was not at all sure what window-shopping was, the boy obediently followed Fred's lead. In Shaftesbury Avenue, Fred entered a large music shop with an awe-struck Stimpo at his heels and said to an assistant, 'My young friend here would like an electric guitar – something decent and reasonably priced. What have you got that meets that criteria?'

Still firmly believing that he was dreaming, Stimpo left the shop the proud owner of a Broadway Guyatone solid-bodied electric guitar, which had been purchased for him by kind-hearted Fred Cottrell. Stimpo used the guitar during his audition and gave a competent if nervous demonstration of his instrumental talent, after which a recording engineer thanked him for his time and interest. Neither Fred nor Stimpo were contacted by the studios in the days that followed, but both agreed that it had been a never-to-be forgotten experience.

The Bandits played at the Teenbeat Club on many occasions and, whilst these performances were in fact the band's only public appearances, they were useful in 'show casing' the boys' individual and collective talent – John Wilmington being the first to attract the attention of another band. He took up an offer to join the locally-based Jaguars, and was replaced by Ian Jay. Some time after, drummer Jeff Walbridge filled a vacancy created by Ray Hewitt.

Largely due to the general economic climate, the Teenbeat Club was closed down in the late fifties, the contents of Fred Cottrell's wallet immediately returning to something approaching normal, and with the demise of the club, came the break-up of The Bandits. It is not known whether Sid Johnston played again, but the paths of Stimpo, Mike Tozer, Ian Jay and Jeff Walbridge were to cross once more, in a band called the Tornadoes.

In January 1961, Stimpo, now twenty years old, was contacted by Mike Tozer who asked him if he would like to listen to a new band that he was currently singing with. On entering the youth club at Park Lodge, Stimpo was greeted by Mike, Ian Jay and Jeff Walbridge. Introducing him to rhythm guitarist Dave Martin, Mike Tozer informed him that these old, and new, friends did in fact constitute his new band, the Tornadoes.

'Who's the lead guitarist then?' asked Stimpo.
'You are,' replied Mike.

From the outset, Stimpo felt comfortable with the band. The weekly rehearsal was always really good fun and whilst he had enjoyed playing skiffle, he loved playing rock and roll – it had so much drive and energy. Given the time, and with a lot of hard work, he believed the Tornadoes possessed the capability to become a very good outfit. Ken Cavanagh thought so too…

From Yeovil, an agent for a large insurance company, Ken Cavanagh had heard the Tornadoes at a social club in the town and thought, like Stimpo, that the boys had potential. After the dance had ended, Ken introduced himself and offered to manage the band. He told the boys that he was well connected in the music business, and felt sure that with their co-operation he could further their careers. Within a few weeks of their acceptance of Ken's offer, the lads were convinced that they had made the correct decision when he informed them that they were going to London.

Manager Ken Cavanagh getting his point across. l–r: Ken Cavanagh, Mike Tozer, Roadie Ivor Martin, Steve Stimpson, Ian Jay, Dave Martin, Rod Trott.

Ken had arranged a matinée booking at the Nuffield Centre and an evening engagement at the famous 2-I's coffee bar in Old Compton Street. Haunt of some of the top names in the pop industry, together with scores of young hopefuls, the 2-I's had been the launch pad for Cliff Richard, The Shadows, Marty Wilde and many more. On the evening of 4 November 1961 the Tornadoes were to be the support act for American singer Vince Taylor and his band.

The big day dawned. An assortment of cars, the majority of which were roadworthy, left Yeovil and set off for the nation's capital. Arriving mid-morning, Ken Cavanagh, who had planned the trip to the last detail, guided the little convoy to a parking zone in Frith Street – just around the corner from Old Compton Street. The boys then enjoyed a hearty brunch at a small café during which Ken laid down some ground rules.

'Right you lot, listen to me. I know that you want to go sightseeing and I appreciate the fact that you are all fully grown men and not children, but I have to emphasise that tonight's gig could be your big chance – so don't blow it!'

'We'll go and have a look at the 2-I's when you've finished your meal, then you can do your own thing. We'll meet back here at one o'clock sharp – we've got to be at the Nuffield Centre by two. The nearest tube station is at Tottenham Court Road, and one more thing – this is Soho, if you should be approached by a young lady who asks you if you'd like a nice time, bear in mind that she's not offering to take you to the pictures!'

Stimpo remembers that they walked the short distance from Frith Street to the 2-I's where Ken sought out the manager. In his absence the boys waited and took in the atmosphere, which even in the hours of daylight, was electric. Ken returned some five minutes later and said to the boys, 'That's all settled, we're meeting Vince Taylor at six o'clock to sort out playing times. You can use his band's amplifiers, drum kit and PA system, so you only need to bring your guitars. Ok, off you go – have a good time and behave yourselves.'

Ken was pleased and perhaps a little relieved, when the boys reported as instructed to the café at one o'clock on the dot. At the Nuffield Centre, the lads were surprised to see three brand new Vox amplifiers complete with dust covers adorning the front of the stage. 'Are we double-handed this afternoon, Ken?' asked Stimpo.

'No,' said Ken with a grin, 'I bought them last week and had them delivered here so that you could use them this afternoon.'

At the 2-I's, Vince Taylor's road crew were hard at work manhandling and erecting what seemed to the boys from the Westcountry like a ton of equipment, with comparative ease. The roadies had politely refused the Tornadoes' offer of help, indicating in the vernacular that it was more than their jobs were worth to let any Tom, Dick or Harry set the gear up.

The Tornadoes heard rather than saw Vince Taylor enter the room. The American appeared to be engaged in a heated discussion with another man. Arms flailing wildly and clearly agitated, the singer was shouting, 'What a goddamn inconvenient time to be taken ill, where's his commitment, tell him he's fired!' The boys sat flabbergasted as Ken calmly put down his coffee cup, walked across to the American, proffered his right hand and said, 'You must be Vince Taylor, I'm Ken Cavanagh, the manager of the support band, is there anything I can do to help?'

Evidently well schooled in public relations, the star's attitude changed immediately. He explained to Ken that his guitarist had been taken ill and asked if the Tornadoes' lead guitarist could help out.

Stimpo had a fabulous evening. The Tornadoes played as well as they had ever done, and he more than adequately coped with the hastily rehearsed Vince Taylor numbers. Vince brought to the notice of the cheering audience the fact that Stimpo had stepped-in at the very last minute, and added his own tribute. At the end of the evening Vince reiterated his thanks and asked Stimpo if would like to join his band. The band he said was flying to Paris the next day to perform a series of concerts after which they would be touring in the United States until the end of the summer. A flattered but loyal Stimpo referred the singer to Ken Cavanagh who, after giving the matter some consideration, insisted that Stimpo, and indeed the other members of the Tornadoes, were under contract and would not be released.

In August 1962 the Tornadoes completely 're-shuffled the pack'. Ken Cavanagh was promoted by his employer, discovered that his leisure time was at a premium and relinquished the post of manager. Mike Tozer left to form a new band and his departure was followed by that of bass guitarist Ian Jay, and drummer Jeff Walbridge.

The Cortinas. l-r: Dave Martin, Steve Stimpson, Jeff Walbridge, Rod Trott and Ian Jay.

Vocalist Rod Trott joined the two surviving Tornadoes, Dave Martin and Stimpo, and with bassist Mick Francis and drummer Bob Chainey, a new band was formed. The boys discussed the matter of a name for the new band at some length. Mick and Bob thought that the name Tornadoes, now well known in both Somerset and Dorset should be retained. Stimpo disagreed, saying that there were several good reasons for changing the name. Firstly, a professional band called the Tornados had just released a record called Telstar, which was already in the charts. Secondly, there was a group in Exeter called the Tornadoes fronted by a guy called Gary Kane who had recently been featured in *South West Scene* magazine, who had apparently been around for years, and lastly, Mike Tozer came up with the name originally and he might want to use it for his new band.

Dave Martin agreed with Stimpo, and suddenly said, 'How about calling the band the Cortinas?' Initially, Dave's suggestion was met with cries of, 'What's

The Tornadoes at the New Hall, Tiverton. l–r: Jeff Walbridge, Sid Johnston, Steve Stimpson, and high-kicking Mike Tozer.

a Cortina – You what – and Eh?' Dave explained that his father, Ivor, was in the motor trade, and had been telling him about a new model Ford motor car called the Cortina.

'Oh, it's a car. Well that's all right then,' responded Rod Trott. 'Yeah, the Cortinas – I like that, it's kinda sexy.' Mentally, Dave Martin thought that Rod's reaction might have been a little different had the car in question been a Humber Super Snipe.

Returning briefly to their roots by accepting bookings in village halls in the immediate area, luck favoured the Cortinas when the band was featured in both the local press and the *County Gazette*. Agents and club secretaries, always on the lookout for new talent and unaware that Mike Tozer was still very much in business, reacted swiftly to the newspaper article. The band became exceptionally busy and was well regarded by other musicians. Indeed there were many times when the somewhat haughty attitude of one or two professional artists, with whom the Cortinas were sharing the stage, became laughable.

The addition of a Ford Transit van, supplied and occasionally serviced by Ivor Martin, enabled the band to accept engagements not only in Somerset, but throughout the South West. The boys were regular visitors to the Civic Hall in Exeter where, in the High Street, ironically just one day before Ian was due to service the van, the near-side front door fell off.

From Shaftesbury to Sidmouth, Bournemouth to Boscastle, the Cortinas supported many of the great touring acts: Freddie and the Dreamers, The Searchers, and The Hollies at Glastonbury and Salisbury Town Halls – and at Tavistock Town Hall, Gary Brooker's amazing Procol Harum.

The Cortinas. l-r: Mick Francis, Rod Trott, Bob Chainey, Tony Hawkins and Steve Stimpson.

Steve 'Stim' Stimpson.

In the two exciting years between the band's formation and the break-up at the end of 1964, changes to the line-up were few and involved the lead vocalist only. Rod Trott left the band to further his song-writing career. At the time of writing Rod is, and has been for many years, one of the UK's finest and most sought-after lyricists.

Singer Tony Hawkins, who had joined the band as a second vocalist with Rod Trott, gave the outfit a wide and varied range of material, and softened the affect of Rod's departure. When, for reasons unknown, Tony decided to leave, Rod was once more able to assist his old friends by introducing his brother Colin who became the outfit's last vocalist.

Author's Note.
As a boy, Steve 'Stimpo' Stimpson wanted nothing more than to be a good citizen in his adopted country. Emotionally scarred, and afflicted with a potentially fatal disease, Stimpo won the battle. During the research into the rock and roll scene in and around the Yeovil area, I have been forcefully reminded of the high esteem in which he is held.

The Crusaders, The Bee Sounds and The Soundimension

'Hello, hello, hello, what's all the noise then, Margaret?'

'Good morning dear, did you sleep well; it was only the postman; he was early today – there's a letter for you on the sideboard. It looks important so you'd better open it straightaway.'

'Right ho!'

'Well, what does it say? Not bad news I hope.'

'Quite the contrary m'dear, I've been promoted to sergeant and I'm to take charge of the station in Somerton – it'll mean uprooting again of course, but I expect you're getting used to that by now.'

Within three weeks of receiving the news of his promotion, former police constable William Beer, his wife Margaret and son John, moved into the house adjacent to the police station in Market Square, Somerton – the ancient capital of Wessex.

Born in Lulsgate near Bristol Airport, John Beer, due entirely to his father's vocation, had since birth resided in the Long Ashton area of Bristol, Frome, Weston-super-Mare and Bridgwater. On settling in Somerton, John became a pupil of Huish Episcopi Secondary Modern School. His homework however was often 'interrupted' by the sound of music filtering through the windows of the White Hart Hotel next door. Further investigation by the twelve-year-old music lover revealed that a skiffle group called The Railroaders was responsible for the noise. The four members of the little band, rhythm guitarist and vocalist Mike Mitchell, bass player Reg Burt, drummer Peter Perry and lead guitarist Graham Keats were amiable enough, and raised no objection to John's polite request that he be permitted to listen to them rehearsing. John became a fixture at each practice session, inevitably arriving before anyone else.

John Beer.

Toward the end of the 'fabulous fifties', The Railroaders 'went electric' and changed their name. Mike Mitchell adopted the stage name Mike Slain and the band became The Vikings. If he had been interested previously John Beer was now totally enthralled, and made a mental note to learn both how to play the guitar and how to build and maintain his own amplifier. Lead guitarist Graham Keats set him on the road to achieving his first goal by teaching him a few chords and allowing the boy to practise them on his Hofner guitar during a break in the proceedings.

Shortly after the purchase of his new Hofner Colorama guitar, rhythm guitarist Mike Mitchell (aka Mike Slain) left the band to get married. Like the majority of musicians, especially guitarists, Mike did not possess unlimited funds and sold his guitar to help finance his forthcoming nuptials. The good news as far as teenager John Beer was concerned, was that the guitar was purchased by his mum Margaret and given to him as an early Christmas present; the bad news being that the guitar was solid-bodied – which meant that it required an amplifier to make it audible, and Mum was not about to spend more of her hard-earned housekeeping money on the purchase of an amplifier.

Mulling things over in his mind, John's thoughts turned to his old friend Harry Crabb. An electronics engineer employed at the EMI factory in Wookey Hole near the cathedral city of Wells, Harry was consulted with a view to introducing John to the vagaries of electronics. With his mentor overseeing every move, the boy contrived to build his own amplifier with which to power his electric guitar. The resulting 10 watts output amplifier, little bigger than a wireless, worked surprisingly well much to the amazement of his Mum and Dad.

Following Mike Mitchell's exit from the band, which in deference to the Red Lion pub where rehearsals were now held had been renamed the Rocking Red Lions, John was invited to become the rhythm guitarist. An induction was not deemed necessary – John knew the words and chords to all of the band's repertoire, unbeknown to lead guitarist, Graham. Ironically, it was this knowledge, coupled with both confidence and competence, which ultimately led to his being ousted from the band.

John's recruitment had solved one of the Lions' two immediate problems – they were once again fully staffed in the instrumental department. The services of a good vocalist, however, continued to be a priority matter. Auditions were held in the Red Lion's self-contained dance hall to the rear of the premises, but none of the would-be singers met the band's seemingly simple criteria – that of being able to sing in tune. Drummer Peter Perry annulled this particular complication. Throughout the time that Mike Mitchell had been the group's lead singer, Peter had warbled happily and acoustically from his comparatively innocuous position behind the guitar-playing front line, with neither microphone nor inclination to sing anything other than backing vocals. He did in fact have a fine voice – a fact that had not been lost on his colleagues, and he was eventually persuaded to 'front' the band, albeit from the back.

The occasional booking at a local youth club or village hall together with a substantial amount of overtime work by his father, and the trading-in of the Hofner, made possible the purchase of a Burns Artist guitar and a Bird 'Golden Eagle' amplifier. Some months later, in the absence of any current Rocking Red Lions engagements, John reverted back to the ploy – tried and tested by countless musicians over many years – and 'tapped-up' dad for an additional loan.

Whilst his parents' monetary outlay was almost certainly never fully reimbursed, John did repay their faith in his ability. In addition to learning and memorising more complicated chord shapes, he began to pick out the melody-line of songs and instrumental pieces popular at that time – initially on a single string but later utilising all six. Previously beset by the constant strumming of chords, Mum and Dad Beer were now able to recognise the tune (most of the time anyway). At subsequent Red Lions rehearsals, the meticulous and detailed analysis of each tune or song that John learnt was, with the possible exception of lead guitarist Graham, admired and well received by the other members of the band.

In fairness to Graham, being a working man he had substantially less leisure time available in which to practise, he had to acknowledge that the young pretender was getting pretty darned good. There is of course only one king in every castle, and John's newly-found skills quickly became available on a free transfer…

Author's Note.

The characteristics of the musicians comprising what is generally accepted as being a traditional group line-up i.e. rhythm guitarist, bass guitarist, drummer, and lead guitarist, have over the years been subject to scrutiny, and this has led to the following conclusions being reached:

Rhythm guitarists – stoic, and endowed with a good, if not encyclopaedic memory, they rarely get excited.

Bass guitarists – usually shy and dead sensible. Teachers or professional people with a few bob stashed away who always fancied being a lead guitarist, but didn't want to stand out in a crowd.

Drummers – they just destroy things don't they?

Lead guitarists – extrovert in the extreme, they leap about like Benzedrine-fuelled kangaroos. Sometimes referred to as 'the flash git on the end'.

The Crusaders. l–r: Ray Thyer, John Beer, Mike Tilley, Mike Gillett.

Unable to locate a band with a deficit in the lead or rhythm guitarist department, John took the decision to form his own band. Recently demobbed from the Army, Mike Tilley from Langport had played guitar during his service years, and had been an avid supporter of The Railroaders, Vikings and Rocking Red Lions when home on leave. He became a recruit for the second time in his life when he teamed up with John Beer in the Crusaders – this being the name chosen by John to identify Somerton's latest pop sensation.

A volunteer bass player was forthcoming in Mike Gillett. A friend of both John and Mike Tilley, Mike Gillett lived in Kingsdon, near Somerton, where his parents owned a grocery shop. In the first instance Mike 'faked-up' a bass guitar from bits and pieces, but soon graduated to a Hofner solid.

Bringing up the rear, so to speak, was farm worker and part-time grave digger Ray Thyer. Ray, yet another supporter of the Rocking Red Lions from the early days, had long dreamed of playing the drums in a band. Revealing his ambition to Mike Tilley, he was delighted when Mike invited him to join the group and promptly bought himself an inexpensive, but adequate drum kit.

Playing merely for pleasure, the Crusaders amassed a sizeable library of instrumentals. Two factors governed the band's choice of material. First, the band had no vocalist and second, John's guitar skills and accumulated knowledge made the task of learning the tunes relatively simple for the other members.

'Quill', the nickname bestowed on Mike Tilley by some schoolfriends, having done a first-class public-relations job on Ray Thyer, was also responsible for the enlistment of two vocalists. Mike's brother and sister, Nigel and Sandra, frequently listened to the Crusaders practising in the front room of their parents' home and to be frank, were both of the opinion that, whilst the instrumentals sounded fine, the boys were making a right pig's ear of the vocals.

Sandra's soft tones were in stark contrast to those of her brother whose raw, gutsy voice was often compared to that of Animals lead singer Eric Burdon. The differing qualities of the siblings' voices gave the Crusaders enormous flexibility in their selection of material. The volume generated by the six-piece outfit, not to mention overcrowding, eventually compelled the band to move its practice venue to the village hall at Kingsdon. The group's first red-letter day came when they performed at the Ace of Clubs near St Mary's Church in Blake Square, Bridgwater. Filled to capacity with workers from the power station at Hinckley Point, the Crusaders fully deserved their fee of £8.

The Crusaders' flight of fancy received another boost when Langport-based market trader and café owner Tony Pomeroy offered to become their manager. Tony had listened to the group at the Ace of Clubs and had thoroughly enjoyed the music. He was convinced that his entrepreneurial skills could further the band's ascent of the semi-professional ladder. A larger-than-life character, Tony numbered among his many friends a gentleman by the name of Ralph Stanford. Ralph, the brother of Trevor (who will no doubt be better known as piano-playing superstar Russ Conway), was able to furnish Tony with invaluable contact information which greatly assisted his managerial mission.

Tony's dedication and obdurate belief in both his own ability and the band's talent, took the Crusaders from the relative obscurity of village halls and youth clubs, to more prestigious venues like Butlins Holiday Camp in Minehead, the Winter Gardens Pavilion in Weston-super-Mare, and the Webbington Country Club near Axbridge. The latter proved to be extremely memorable…

At Tony's insistence, dress suits replaced shirts and jeans, and new amplification was purchased – thus transforming not only the look of the band, but also the sound. The Crusaders reached the intermission at the Webbington 'on something of a high'. An appreciative audience had given the boys a warm welcome, which greatly assisted in calming their 'first night' nerves. There had in fact been only one glitch in the entire performance when, during a quieter number and for reasons unknown, John Beer's spanking new Selmer amplifier loudly broadcast the fact that Sierra Oscar Two-Three had arrived at his, her, or its destination.

With a working knowledge of valve amplifiers, John knew that this happened on occasions – it was something to do with comparable frequencies and, although annoying, had no adverse affect on the electronic circuitry. Nevertheless, John decided that he would use his old amplifier during the second half, and strolled out to the van to fetch it. On reaching the van he discovered that it had been blocked in on all four sides by other vehicles. Access through the two front doors was impossible without standing on the bonnet of one of the adjacent cars, and access to the rear of the van was similarly restricted by an elderly Austin A30 two-door saloon. He did however notice that there was plenty of room behind the little Austin, and that the front quarterlight in the offside door was ajar. Sliding his hand through the small window, he released the locking mechanism and gently opened the door. Leaning inside he gave the gear stick a tentative shake, slipped the handbrake, and the rest was easy. John pushed the vehicle back a couple of metres and closed the door. On the grounds that the Austin had hardly been secure in the first place, he neither locked the car nor applied the handbrake.

He glanced at his luminous watch in the half-light, there were only ten minutes left before the band began its second set. There was no time to lose. John unlocked the rear doors, leapt into the back of the van, and grabbed his spare amplifier. As he turned to exit the van, he saw to his horror that the little A30 had silently rolled across the smooth tarmacadam surface of the car park, and was about to roll down the steep embankment to the lower level of the split-level car park. John dropped his amplifier and ran to the vehicle.

The Bee Tones. l–r: Mike Tilley, ?, John Lacey, John Beer, Bob Patey.

Well… almost to the vehicle. There was little that he could do. The Austin gained momentum, and came to rest atop the bonnet of a two-year-old Volvo.

To his credit, John immediately reported the incident to the hotel receptionist, and admitted that he had both moved the vehicle and omitted to apply the parking brake. His honesty – assisted by a character reference and a cheque for five hundred pounds from his father – saved him the ignominy of an appearance in court. An apprenticed electrical engineer employed by a gentleman called Cyril Head who ran a little business in Langport, John recalls that it took him almost a year to reimburse his father.

During that year of financial restraint, the Crusaders, to quote John Beer, 'sort of fell apart'. Mike Gillett left on the grounds that he needed a change of direction which, as Mike was a drag-racing fanatic, came as a surprise to everybody, and Mike Tilley refused point-blank to turn professional and accompany the band on a tour of Germany which Tony Pomeroy had arranged with a friend by the name of Dave Dee. The new amplification and public-address system was returned to Radio House in Yeovil from where it had been purchased, and the hire-purchase agreements cancelled. Both frustrated and disappointed with the band's decision, manager Tony Pomeroy severed all links with the outfit.

Following the break up of the Crusaders, John Beer and Mike Tilley kept up their friendship, often playing guitars together in one or the other of their houses. They were subsequently joined by organist John Holland, and a drummer from Street called Mike Haskell who worked for a Glastonbury Timber Company, in forming the Bee Tones.

Playing a blend of instrumentals, pop and traditional dance music, the Bee Tones entertained on the local pub and club circuit with an unchanged line-up for about eighteen months prior to John Holland's decision to return to solo work. His place in the band was taken by a pianist from Street called

Soundimension. l–r: Standing: Jim Green, Terry Culliford and John Beer. Seated: John Lacey.

Bob Patey. Nominally a 'honky-tonk' pub-style piano player, Bob was kindly permitted to use John Holland's Vox Continental organ until he acquired his own instrument. John Lacey, formerly the drummer with Eddie Dark and The Salvoes, became a member of the band at the departure of Mike Haskell, and the band changed its name to Soundimension.

In addition to their own gigs with Soundimension, John Beer and John Lacey regularly 'depped' with a band from the Chard and Ilminster areas called The Marksmen. The situation however was both impractical and unworkable. Something had to give, and The Marksmen disbanded. The break-up of the band proved fortuitous for Soundimension as it coincided with bass guitarist Mike Tilley's announcement to call it a day, and allowed Jim Green (the former vocalist and rhythm guitarist with The Marksmen), to step into his shoes. Bass guitarist Mike 'Mick' Smitten – a time-served member of the Fleet Air Arm stationed at Yeovilton completed the jigsaw.

John Beer fondly remembers this line-up as being the most musically proficient. Soundimension was able to fulfil the outstanding Bee Tones' bookings, and these engagements more than adequately showcased the band's undoubted talent. Soundimension's ancient Ford Thames van could regularly be seen throughout Somerset and Dorset – Portland Prison Officers' Club being one of their favourite venues.

In later years, the band's well-drilled polished performances were further enhanced by the addition of Glastonbury keyboard player Terry Culliford. Had John Beer not moved to the village of Westleigh on the Devon–Somerset border in 1976, Soundimension would undoubtedly have continued well into the eighties.

John continues to entertain, occasionally 'depping' with Monopole, but more often than not as one-half of a country duo, with his wife Shirley.

Soundimension at HM Prison Officers' Club at Portland. l–r: Mick Smitten, Jim Green, John Beer, John Lacey.

The Germs also known as The Popeyes

In 1962, Brian Epstein became the manager of The Beatles, the musical careers of Otis Redding and Stevie Wonder began, and Allan Boobyer bought his first guitar from his girlfriend Elaine Cattle who dumped him a few weeks later.

A sixth-form student at Huish's Grammar School in Taunton, Allan, nicknamed 'Booze' by one of his schoolmates after drinking a full bottle of Tizer without pausing for breath, regularly visited the home of fellow student Tim Poole in Northfield Avenue, near French Weir, to listen to Tim's large collection of vinyl records.

Guitarist Booze Boobyer and drummer Keith Boobyer at the County Ballroom, Taunton.

'Garage Music'. l–r: Tim Poole, Dave Hembrow, Booze Boobyer.

A guitarist, Tim owned an Ormston Burns solid-bodied instrument and a diminutive Watkins Westminster amplifier. Fleet-fingered, he was able to play the melody-line to a number of tunes that would have taxed even the most experienced guitarist. His personal favourite was a tune called the 'Popeye Twist'. Written by Clem Cattini the drummer of the Tornadoes, the 'Popeye Twist' was a variation on the Sailor's Hornpipe much beloved by promenaders on the last night of their concert season. Heavily influenced by Chuck Berry, Duane Eddy, Rhet Stoller and Judd Proctor, Tim's problem lay in playing chords – he seemed to be able to get neither head nor fingers around them. 'Booze', on the other hand, had mastered the majority of major, minor, and seventh chords, but would not have been able to pick out the tune had his life depended on it. The marriage of the two boys' individual skills was therefore well suited.

It is said that every cloud has a silver lining… When his aunt passed away, Booze was bequeathed a small sum of money from her estate. This windfall,

Robin Carey and Booze Boobyer at Wilton Parish Hall.

together with the proceeds from the sale of his Dinky Toy collection, enabled him to buy his first electric guitar – a Broadway solid, and the small Watkins amplifier previously owned by Tim Poole who had upgraded to a Watkins Dominator. His friend's acquisition of the equipment prompted Tim to suggest that drummer Dave Hembrow be approached, and a group formed.

The son of a garage proprietor in East Reach, Taunton, and like Tim and Booze a student at Huish's Grammar School, Dave had owned his drum kit for some time and had been awaiting the opportunity to join a band. His father, Les, whilst not wishing to stand in the way of his son's leisure activities, was concerned that the band, by virtue of the late evening–early morning routine followed by musicians in the normal course of events, would affect his son's strict training regime. Dave liked to swim…

At six o'clock each morning come rain or shine, Dave could be found at the local swimming pool. An exceptional athlete, he had represented his school at both primary and senior level, and was an automatic choice for all inter-county competitions. His swimming-coach had stated publicly that with continued hard work and determination, David would almost certainly be selected for the national squad to represent his country at the next Olympic Games, which were to be staged in Tokyo two years hence. Dave was quick to reassure his sceptical father that the band would not in any way compromise his training. 'In fact,' he continued, 'you can come to all the practices if you like, and the gigs – as soon as we get some bookings. Then you'll know that I'm home on time.'

Having heard his son beating seven bells out of his drum kit on a number of occasions, Les thought it highly unlikely that anyone would be daft enough to part with their hard-earned money in order to hear him play, and asked where the practices were to be held. Dave replied that he and the boys were rather hoping that they could use the service bay at the garage in East Reach. 'We could shunt a few cars about – flip the inspection ramp up, and use the space underneath.'

Les felt a shiver go up the back of his neck as he envisaged his son and his two pals manoeuvring several thousands of pounds worth of customers' vehicles around in a confined space. 'I'll do any shunting that needs to be done,' said Les quickly. 'Better still, you can use the spray-shop – it's empty at the moment. I'll drive you down there and pick you up later.'

It very soon became obvious to The Popeyes (the selected name for the band, which enabled Tim's party-piece the 'Popeye Twist' to become the signature tune), that they badly needed a bass guitarist – and Rob Carey seemed to be just the chap.

Rob arrived at Huish's Grammar School mid-term. His father, a major in the Army, had been posted with his family from Kenya in Africa, to Sherford Camp in Trull Road, Taunton. Art being one of Rob's chosen GCE A-level subjects, he was placed in the same tutor group as Booze. Aware that the first day in a new school or college can be daunting, Allan introduced himself and the two became friends. He told Rob that he played in a group called The Popeyes, and invited him to the next rehearsal. Rob said that he loved the music that the current crop of bands were recording and wished that he were able to play an instrument of some kind.

Coerced by smooth-talking Booze, Rob parted with some money that he had been given as a birthday present in purchasing an inexpensive bass guitar. Without a suitable amplifier the solid-bodied bass was inaudible anywhere other than in a Trappist monastery, and thus about as useful as a gearbox in a glider. Bereft of funds after buying the bass, Rob was helped out by Booze's father Len who, by signing a hire-purchase form, acquired a bass amplifier on the boy's behalf.

Tim and Booze assumed joint responsibility for Rob's tuition in the gentle art of bass playing. Tim touched upon the rudiments of music, explained how the instrument was tuned and demonstrated a twelve-bar blues. Booze's approach was somewhat more simplistic. Strumming the chord of A major, he said to Rob, 'When I play this chord,' he paused momentarily then pointed to the third string on the bass, 'you hit that note!'

The Popeyes' first public engagement, at the Trident Community Centre in Taunton, proved to be a memorable evening. Len Boobyer, Les Hembrow, and Rob Carey's mother had been appointed as temporary roadies until such time as one or more of the boys had passed his driving test, and offspring and equipment were duly transported to the venue. A cursory glance at the electrical sockets at the rear of the small stage revealed that the band's ampli-fication was fitted with the wrong plugs. The problem was solved by removing plugs of the correct denomination from a tea urn, a vacuum cleaner and an old valve wireless found in the kitchen, and fitting them to the amplifiers.

Having satisfied himself that the boys and equipment were okay, Les Hembrow turned to his son and said, 'I'm going to whiz on back now – I've got a stack of paperwork to do. Len tells me that the dance finishes at ten o'clock sharp so I'll be back at about a quarter to ten. Don't hang about afterwards – you've got a training session at six o'clock tomorrow morning.'

Les returned to the hall at five past ten to find the band in full cry. Striding forcefully through the crowd he stood to the side of the stage and looked meaningfully at his son while tapping the face of his watch. Spotting Les out of the corner of his eye and realising that the band had over-run, Tim Poole brought the instrumental to a close. Mouthing his apologies to his father, Dave sprang to his feet, swiftly packed his drums away and was gone. The remaining trio of Booze, Tim and Rob played two more numbers – one of which was the last waltz, and brought the event to a much tidier conclusion.

On the Monday morning following the Thursday evening dance, Booze, Rob and Dave Hembrow were summoned from their respective tutorials by the

Headmaster, Mr Peel-Corbin. The Head was at pains to inform them that, in his opinion, midweek bookings with the beat group would do their studies no good at all. He went on to extol the virtues of a healthy mind and body, and the efficacious properties of a good night's sleep. The boys never discovered how Mr Peel-Corbin had 'got wind' of the midweek booking.

Rob left the band at the start of 1964 to further his education at the Taunton Art College (now the Somerset College of Art and Technology), and was replaced by a young man called Chris Sayer. Formerly with a local outfit called The Ravens, Chris was introduced to Booze Boobyer at the Cross Keys public house in Taunton, by his younger brother, Stuart. Booze had watched The Ravens on many occasions, was a great admirer of the bass guitarist's skills, and was both surprised and delighted when Chris accepted his invitation to join The Popeyes.

At a hastily arranged rehearsal, his first with The Popeyes, Chris said that he had for some time been contemplating a change of direction musically, and Booze's invitation had been timely. Chris continued by saying that he thought the name of the band was a bit dated, and that it should be changed to reflect the new line-up and repertoire...

   'What we need,' Chris said airily, 'is a name that's snappy and infectious.'
   Tim laughed. 'Like a nasty germ you mean.'

During the following ten-month period, The Germs underwent an almost complete transformation. Red silk shirts and silver 'kipper' ties were purchased from The Shirt Shop in Billet Street, Taunton, conveniently owned by a friend of Booze Boobyer. Instrumentals were replaced by covers of current chart material, although Tim insisted that he be allowed to play the 'Popeye Twist' occasionally, and the band adopted a more professional attitude generally. Business cards, designed and produced by Booze and

The Germs. l–r: Booze Boobyer, Chris Sayer, Tim Poole, Keith Boobyer.

Chris, were freely distributed at gigs, and were largely responsible for the interest shown in the band by local promoters Brian Mapstone and Don Culliford.

By courtesy of Brian Mapstone, the highly-respected boss of Westside Promotions, The Germs regularly appeared at the town hall in Glastonbury, and the large village hall at Coxley. Taunton agent Don Culliford provided a great deal of work for The Germs both locally and in the Bridgwater area, but rarely advertised the outfit correctly, invariably calling the band The Grems.

Dave Hembrow left the band in 1965 to attend Loughborough College, arguably the country's finest sporting academy. His place was taken by former Avalons drummer Keith Boobyer – a cousin to Germs rhythm guitarist Booze. Vastly experienced, Keith quickly negated any concerns that the boys may have had on 'losing' Dave Hembrow. Probably the band's busiest year, 1965 was filled with noteworthy events…

Booked as the support band to the Graham Bond Organisation at the annual Arts Ball, held in the County Ballroom in Taunton, The Germs were declared the most popular of the two outfits by the massive crowd. The audience voted, as they say, with their feet, by leaving the room shortly after the 'Organisation's' opening number, only to return when the local band once again took the stage.

At the Black Horse public house in Bridgwater, the boys continued to play whilst a 'punch-up' that made the battle of the Little Bighorn seem like a petty squabble was in full swing. Men and women, even the landlord were trading punches with a man who, the boys guessed, would not appear on the landlord's Christmas card list that year. The local police were called to the scene and sensibly waited until the troublemakers were either unconscious or just plain bored, before moving to restore order.

At the start of the next year, the year in which England were to win the Jules Rimet trophy, Tim Poole decided that he no longer got a buzz from playing with the band and called it a day. Allan, Chris and Keith continued to perform as a trio for a further twelve months – although for half of this period, the boys were assisted by talented guitarist and vocalist Pete Bendall who had worked with several bands in the Taunton area, the most recent being the In-Pact.

The advent of mobile and resident discotheques appeared to apply the kiss of death to the fortunes of the band. Following a spell of three weeks during which the boys had received neither enquiry nor confirmed booking, The Germs disbanded.

Chris Sayer formed his own three-piece outfit, which he named the Somerset String Ensemble; with Tim Poole on lead guitar, Ken Ostler – from Chris's old band The Ravens – on rhythm guitar, and Chris himself on bass guitar. The SSE was unusual in that it did not have a drummer.

ODEON POLL WINNERS'
AWARD
1966

This is to certify that **The Germs...**
has been elected **The most exciting New Group** in the 1966 Odeon Teen Club P.W.

.... by **The Management of the ODEON**

Fancy that! l–r: Booze Boobyer, Chris Sayer, Pete Bendall.

Keith Boobyer became a freelance drummer, the majority of his work being with traditional dance bands. Booze, after a break of six months, joined the James Allen Band as a bass guitarist. The band, taking its name from bandleader and drummer James 'Jim' Best and his son Alan, held a residency at Blue Waters Holiday Camp in Seaton, East Devon, during the summer season, and was constantly in demand on the local circuit throughout the rest of the year. In truth, Booze found the less frenetic style of the band very much to his liking, and the friendships formed with accordionist Bill Duddridge and occasional saxophonist Fred Knighton became a permanent source of comfort and encouragement.

The Somerset String Ensemble.

The Blackdown Hills are alive, to the sound of music…

Not unique by any means – it is certainly unusual to find four members of the same family performing in a musical group on a purely amateur basis. Self-taught pianist John 'Jack' Chard played, solely for his own amusement, in the front room of the house that he shared with his wife, sons and daughters at Crosslands, in the Tone Dale area of Wellington. Perhaps 'pub pianist' most adequately describes Jack's style of playing, but nonetheless there was not a tune written that Jack, having heard the melody once, could not play within a few minutes. The financial constraints of raising and supporting a wife and family limited Jack's leisure time, and visits to his local for the odd pint were restricted to one evening per week, to which he greatly looked forward.

On Saturday evenings, the Eight Bells public house in High Street, Wellington frequently 'employed' the services of a gentleman called Jim Lochrie who, together with his accordion and banjo, would entertain the clientele in the saloon bar. Lucky locals were usually treated to a selection of wartime songs – never to be forgotten classics such as 'We're Going to Hang out the Washing on the Seigfried Line', 'Kiss Me Goodnight Sergeant Major' and 'Run Rabbit Run'. These diamonds in the jewellery box of musical history were invariably followed by more modern items from celebrated recording artists such as Max Bygraves and Alma Cogan. Jack and his family enjoyed their Saturday evenings at the Eight Bells, and Jim Lochrie became a good friend.

In 1969, Jack's youngest son Alan, a quiet, rather reserved young man, bought himself an inexpensive acoustic guitar and a 'Teach Yourself' book with some money that he had received for his birthday. Perhaps not sur-prisingly, bearing in mind his father's natural talent, he could play many of the more commonly used chords within a few weeks. His elder brother Garry, who had long harboured a dream to sing with a band professionally, was at first, as far as Alan was concerned, a bit of a pain, almost bullying him into accompanying his vocals. But Alan was under no illusions as to the quality of his brother's voice, being well aware that Garry had auditioned for the vocalist's job with top local outfit The Storm, and had spent a few months singing with a band called Eternity Road in the company of his great friend, bass player Paul 'Jess' Jordan, drummer Peter James, and a fine keyboard player called Trevor Bright.

By the summer of the following year, Jack and his wife Ellen, his three daughters Angela, Hazel and Sheila, and the two boys, had moved across town – from Crosslands to Priory. Alan had mastered many of the most commonly used chords, effortlessly changing from one to another with no deviation in tempo. Additionally, Alan had discovered that he could sing the harmony or descant line to Garry's lead vocal, and whilst his voice lacked the power of that possessed by his brother, it was nevertheless well pitched and tonally pleasing.

Ever supportive of his sons' efforts, Jack Chard mentioned their prowess to Jim Lochrie. On the Chard family's next Saturday night out at the Eight Bells, Jim invited Garry and Alan to sing a couple of songs whilst he took a short break. The spontaneous applause, whistles, and cries of 'encore' that rang around the bar following their performance, and the congratulatory pats on the back as they returned to their seats, remain a fond memory.

At the dinner table the next day, between mouthfuls of roast pork and apple-sauce, Jack again praised his two sons on their performance.

'The landlord wants us to sing every Saturday,' said Garry, 'but I told him that the customers would soon get bored – listening to the same thing every week.'

'What did he say to that?' asked Jack.

'Come in whenever you can,' said Alan.

'We'll have to get an electric guitar and an amplifier first,' suggested Garry. 'I could hardly hear Al last night.'

Addressing his father, Alan said, 'Why don't you join in on the piano Dad, that would boost the sound.'

'I suppose it would,' replied Jack, 'I'll give it some thought.'

Jack awoke from his post-lunch nap to find that he and Ellen were alone in the house.

'Where is everybody?' he asked.

'Garry and Alan have gone over to Jess Jordan's to tell him about last night,'

Home Brew. l–r: Alan Chard, Garry Chard, Jack Chard, Paul 'Jess' Jordan.

replied Ellen. 'I've no idea where the girls are.'

'What do you think about Alan's idea, me playing piano – with him and Garry I mean,' continued Jack.

'I think it's a lovely idea,' said Ellen, 'and you know you love your music. It'll be like that film with Julie Andrews – where she's a nun looking after those children in Switzerland.'

'I think you'll find it was Austria,' said Jack laughing, 'but I get your drift – umpteen members of the same family singing together, a sort of home-brood.'

'That's what you ought to call the group,' said Ellen, 'Homebrewed. Yes I like that!'

During the next week, Jack purchased a Gem portable organ, a small Marshall amplifier, and a pick-up for Alan's guitar. Both Garry and Alan liked Jack's suggestion to call the trio Homebrewed but thought that 'Homebrew' sounded better.

Young at heart, Jack thoroughly enjoyed the practice sessions in the front room although, as a lover of big-band music, there were times when he had to refrain from expressing his real feelings about some of the songs he was being asked to learn. Jack also found it difficult to adapt his 'pub style' piano playing to that of a group organist. A perfectionist, Jack was adamant that he would not join the boys on stage until he was completely sure that his ability matched theirs. Garry and Alan continued to rehearse with their father on a weekly basis but worked as a duo for almost twelve months before Jack felt sufficiently confident to join them.

When Jack finally became a member of Homebrew, problems were few. The Gem organ now possessed a particularly annoying mains hum which became even more pronounced when the instrument was amplified, but this became slightly less noticeable when Alan's electrified Spanish guitar was connected to an old reel-to-reel tape recorder that was 'blessed' with a similar hum. In addition, the absence of a bass guitarist did little to shore up the trio's rhythm section. Garry had invited his old friend Jess Jordan to join the band but to date he had neither accepted, nor declined the offer.

As a duo, Garry and Alan had appeared at the Cleeve Hotel, the Anchor Inn at Hillfarance, the War Memorial Institute at Rockwell Green, and the Eight Bells public house in Wellington. The boys subsequently revisited all of these venues, but on these occasions they were accompanied by their father, and performed as Homebrew.

Jess Jordan eventually accepted Garry's invitation and lined up with the band for the first time at the War Memorial Institute at Rockwell Green. After the dance, local drummer Tony 'Paddy' Paisley – or 'Pays' as he preferred to be called – a visitor to the Institute that evening and an old friend of Jack Chard, congratulated Jack and the boys on a job well done. The music, he said, had obviously been well rehearsed and had been a pleasure to listen to, but where, Pays wanted to know, was the drummer?

Jack briefly related the history of the band, explaining that they did not yet have a drummer, and asked Pays if he would like the job.

'Well,' replied Pays, 'I'm not playing with any outfit on a permanent basis at the moment and I can't deny that I enjoyed your music, but I've got two or three 'dep' gigs in the diary. What's going to happen if Homebrew isbooked on the same nights?'

'Simple,' said Jack, 'we do exactly what we've done tonight – and play as a four-piece.'

Pays grinned. 'Right then mate, you're on. Let's go and have a drink – you've just got yourself a drummer!'

During the next two years Homebrew, with no changes in personnel, built up a solid following. The ability to adapt its act to suit all age groups made the band an ideal choice for dinner dances. As a consequence, the winter and spring seasons of the year were inordinately busy, as opposed to being just plain busy, during the autumn and summer time.

Grahame Darch.

In 1973, for reasons known only to him, Jess Jordan left the band. A replacement was found almost immediately in Grahame Darch. Formerly the bass guitarist with The Storm, Grahame lived at Crosslands in Wellington, and had known Jack, Garry and Alan for many years. Grahame had not played with a band for a considerable time, but his bass playing at an 'induction' rehearsal was faultless. He loved his bass guitar. It was one of three overwhelming passions in his life, the others being his motorbike and his girlfriend, Stella. Homebrew was back in business!

The final and by far the most attractive addition to the band was Hazel Chard. Sister to Garry and Alan, and second-eldest daughter of Jack, Hazel had a voice to rival her charms. Garry and Alan had from the very beginning tried to persuade her to sing with them, but their overtures were always rebuffed. Around the house Hazel would sing to herself, or to the radio. She would sing along with records on her record player – even to Garry and Alan when they were practising, but she steadfastly refused to sing in public, citing nerves as the reason for her refusal.

Hazel overcame her nerves in 1978 at the birthday party of a family friend, with the assistance of Homebrew, a tambourine, and two glasses – filled to the brim with a colourless Russian liquid. Sitting at a table in the function room of The Heatherton Grange with her mother, her two sisters and several friends, Hazel listened to her brother Garry singing the Don McLean classic from 1972 'American Pie', and thought how good Homebrew was sounding these days. Acknowledging the applause, Garry informed the audience, most of whom he knew, that the band would like to feature his sister Hazel in the next number. Handing her a tambourine, Garry counted the band in and launched into a rock and roll medley. Initially reluctant, Hazel quickly picked up the tempo and joined in. The applause from the party guests and the members of Homebrew that greeted her instrumental debut removed any trace of nerves that she may have had. Returning to her seat she reflected on the last five minutes, and decided that she had really enjoyed herself.

Hazel began rehearsing with the band within days of the birthday party, and remained with them until the band split up – her voice adding a completely new dimension to the sound. The following year, in 1979, Garry, who had been having problems in his private life, left Wellington to live in Weston-super-Mare. The other members of the band, Jack, Alan, Grahame, Pays and Hazel decided that Homebrew would temporarily disband, pending Garry's return.

On his return to Wellington, the band continued as before. Entertainment's agents, club secretaries, and hotel owners were informed that Homebrew was back on the circuit, and once again the offers of work poured in. After six months however, the enthusiasm waned significantly. During Garry's absence, Jack, Alan, Grahame, Pays and Hazel had all discovered that they had hobbies other than the band, which were equally as rewarding, and each booking had now become a chore. Sensibly, Homebrew completed the outstanding engagements and disbanded by mutual consent.

♩ ♫ ♪

The Jaguars latterly known as The Generation

From her slightly elevated position on the dais at the front of the classroom, Joyce Chappell mused as she surveyed her tutor group. The written test that she had set should take no longer than ten minutes to complete and involved nothing more than writing the names of the notes on a pre-printed piece of music. One young girl was gazing out of the window and another stifled a yawn. A tall curly-haired youth at the back of the room who rarely contributed anything to the lesson, sat with both elbows on the lid of his desk, his head in his hands. The thought that he might be asleep, or perhaps dead, momentarily crossed her mind, but even as she watched, the boy vigorously shook his head, picked up his pen and began to write. A charming lady with a progressive attitude to music, Joyce fully understood how her pupils felt about the theory of music. As a lover of the classics and a very fine pianist, she well remembered how complicated the rudiments of music had seemed to her in the early days. Joyce gave the matter a great deal of consideration during the next few days until, finally, she thought she had the answer…

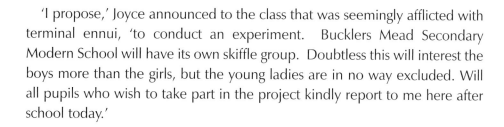

Joyce Peach (née Chappell).

'I propose,' Joyce announced to the class that was seemingly afflicted with terminal ennui, 'to conduct an experiment. Bucklers Mead Secondary Modern School will have its own skiffle group. Doubtless this will interest the boys more than the girls, but the young ladies are in no way excluded. Will all pupils who wish to take part in the project kindly report to me here after school today.'

One of half a dozen boys who returned to the music room that afternoon, John Wilmington loved skiffle, owned a guitar, and could play it. John lived in Allingham Road, just a few doors from one of Yeovil's most popular guitarists Steve Stimpson, by whom he had initially been influenced, and subsequently taught.

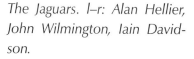

The Jaguars. l–r: Alan Hellier, John Wilmington, Iain Davidson.

BEAT NITE

AT

**THE ROYAL
BRITISH
LEGION
YEOVIL**

WITH

**THE

JAGUARS**

Friday February 8th 1963

8.00pm til 10.30pm   Admission 1/-

The Bucklers Mead skiffle group was a huge success. John and his classmates became mini-celebrities, and were frequently called upon to play at end-of-term dances, the school fete and the Christmas variety show.

In 1958, at the age of fourteen, as described earlier in this book, John teamed up with his mentor Steve Stimpson in a skiffle group called Steve and The Bandits, as the group's rhythm guitarist.

One year later John left school to commence a three-year apprenticeship in hairdressing. He was forewarned that the hours would be long and the wages low. In addition, he was informed that he would be required to spend some time at a training college in Bristol. With regret, John wished the Bandits a fond farewell and walked away.

Employed by Bernard of Mayfair, a hairdressing establishment with a considerable reputation ranking alongside Vidal Sassoon, John was inducted at the shop in Yeovil, and completed two more years of advanced and intensive training at the company's school in Bristol. At the latter end of 1961 John was approached by an excellent young guitarist called Alan Hellier who had for some time wanted to form his own band. Guitarist and apprenticed printer Maurice Briggs, drummer Iain Davidson, and vocalist Rod Trott subsequently joined Alan and John in founding the area's latest rock and roll outfit, The Jaguars.

The band was fortunate in possessing the talents of Alan Hellier and Rod Trott. Alan appeared to be able to play any number that Rod wanted to sing with apparent ease, and Rod, thanks to his astonishing memory, normally knew the lyrics of any number suggested by the band. These two factors made practice sessions both productive and pleasurable.

Tremendous if friendly rivalry existed between The Jaguars and Dale Fender and The Beatmakers, a fact that did not go unnoticed by the pop correspondent of the *Western Daily Press*. This further served to spur The Jaguars' efforts at rehearsals. Timing, volume and overall presentation, were three aspects of the boys' staged performances to which much consideration was given. The Jaguars was an honest band, accepting its limitations but constantly striving to give of its best. In the two years that the band performed as The Jaguars, the boys steadily built up an avid fan base both in Yeovil and throughout South Somerset. Indeed, fans of The Jaguars were most annoyed to read in the *Western Daily Press* that Dale Fender and The Beatmakers were Yeovil's top band. This became a moot point when in 1963, the band was taken under the wing of both Brian Mapstone's Westside Promotions and Frank Huddy's Double 'H' agency.

Ron Trott left the outfit at the end of the year, and his exit was emulated by Maurice Briggs shortly after. The recruitment of a young lad from Yeovil called Richard Parsons then had a profound effect on the band. Richard, an apprenticed barber and classically trained pianist, brought with him immense keyboard skills and a passion for rhythm & blues. The Jaguars became The

Generation and the fans simply loved the change in style. Numbers by Booker T and the MG's and Otis Redding replaced rock and roll standards and became favourites with the ever-increasing army of supporters. The music was innovative and surprisingly popular. With the exception of Minehead-based Justin's Timepiece there were no other bands playing this type of music across the lower reaches of the county and strangely, whether by accident or design, the paths of Timepiece and The Generation never crossed.

Entertainment agents, dance promoters and club secretaries happily discovered that by pairing a rhythm & blues outfit like The Generation with a more conventional rock band on a two-band gig, ticket sales, when compared with those for a two-band event employing the services of two rock groups, increased dramatically – as did the entries in The Generation's diary. Enquiries for the band's services, many of which were subsequently converted into confirmed engagements and duly fulfilled, were received on an almost weekly basis. In addition to a seemingly unlimited supply of local bookings at the Liberal and Labour Clubs in Yeovil, Salisbury and Glastonbury Town Halls to name but four, the boys became regular visitors to the Locarno in Bristol, the Civic Hall in Exeter, and the Great Hall at the University of London. Popular too in the Principality, The Generation frequently crossed the Severn, where their energy and style never failed to please the music-loving teenagers. The Generation could now justifiably claim to be the area's top rhythm & blues outfit.

In 1965, bass guitarist John Wilmington accepted an invitation from his old friend Witold 'Bud' Budzynsky to join The Generation's great rivals The Beatmakers. Shortly to leave the UK on a twelve-month tour of Germany, all the members of The Beatmakers had turned professional except bass player Steve Tucker, hence Bud's recruitment of John. John recalls that the decision to leave The Generation was not an easy one to take, the band after all was successful albeit on an amateur basis, and had achieved much in the last few months. Nevertheless, by using stand-in bass guitarists The Generation continued to delight audiences throughout the Westcountry.

As has already been mentioned in The Beatmakers' biography earlier in this book, John's stay with the band was prematurely truncated by the death of his father. To the delight of Alan, Iain and Richard, John rejoined The Generation at the beginning of October 1966 and remained with the band until its dissolution in 1967. Supporters of the band were sorry to hear that The Generation had left the scene but the same could not be said for the members of the Glastonbury Town Council…

One hugely popular and somewhat raucous song that was included in every Generation performance contained the lyric 'jump'. From the very first time that the band had performed this particular number, vocalist and lead guitarist Alan Hellier had shouted the word rather than sung it, and as if in answer to a command, all the Generation fans in the dance hall had jumped! The song became a feature of each Generation performance, and was especially spectacular upon the wooden, sprung floor at Glastonbury Town Hall. On the occasion of the band's last performance there, Alan's bellowed 'jump' was greeted with a whoop by approximately three hundred fans, all of whom were momentarily airborne, only to come crashing down a split second later.

The letter sent by the Town Council to Westside Promotions made reference to the fact that, despite his best efforts, the caretaker was unable to remove the hundreds of indentations in the floor. The letter continued by saying that the culprits were to be refused entry to all further functions, and that failure to comply with this instruction would certainly lead to the cancellation of all existing and subsequent bookings. Fully aware as to how the damage had been caused, Brian Mapstone, the proprietor of Westside Promotions was torn between laughing and crying. His business was entertainment and he was thrilled to see teenagers enjoying the music supplied by bands that he had booked. He was also, however, aware that there were many other acts, both amateur and professional, who were already booked to appear at the hall.

Left with no option, Brian removed the possibility of Generation fans repeating their impromptu ballet by removing the root cause. Tongue firmly in cheek, Brian informed the boys that there would be no more bookings at the town hall, but that engagements at all other venues would continue as before. There can be little doubt that The Generation possessed the confidence and competence necessary to become a top-flight rhythm & blues band and were, it not for the fact that Alan, Richard, John and Iain were determined to complete their various apprenticeships as an electrician with the Somerset Water Board, barber, hairdresser and printer respectively, would surely have done so.

Justin's Timepiece

The top semi-professional blues band of its day, Justin's Timepiece was formed by Andrew Priddy, Richard Hicks and Mike Fouracre in 1967. Andrew's interest in music and particularly the guitar, stemmed from an instrument fashioned from odd pieces of wood, fishing line, matchsticks and nails which had been constructed by a friend called Tim Porch who, like Andrew, lived in the village of Roadwater. Cossetted by the Brendon Hills, near Washford and but a few miles from Minehead, Roadwater had been home to Andrew from the age of two. The 'Heath Robinson' guitar was a non-starter as a candidate for a Blue Peter badge, but nevertheless Tim was pleased with his creation. He was astounded when, with no knowledge of concert-pitch tunings, Andrew managed to pick out the notes to the Lennon and McCartney song 'Till There Was You'.

Influenced possibly by the much-publicised shenanigans of some very well-known names in the music business, Andrew's father Randolph, a freelance photographer with close links to the media, was somewhat tardy in responding to his son's request that he be given a guitar as a birthday present.

Andrew Priddy.

'He doesn't really want a guitar,' he had said to his wife Thelma. 'It's just a phase he's going through, a fad – he'll forget all about it when he starts at his new school.' The absence of any guitar-shaped gifts on the morning of 19 June 1960 merely strengthened Andrew's resolve to acquire an instrument…

Costing £12, the Watkins Rapier solid-bodied guitar was purchased from a second-hand shop in Minehead, and financed from the proceeds of a traditional craft known as 'trout tickling'.

Author's note. As a former practitioner in the delicate and patience-building art of the foregoing, I am able to write the following with a degree of knowledge gained from many happy hours spent on the banks of the River Exe.

Andrew and a few friends often 'hung out' down by the river during the summer holidays – swimming, playing football and the like. Probably Andrew's best friend, Richard Hicks was keen to try his hand at 'tickling trout' having read an extremely interesting magazine article on survival techniques, whilst sitting in the doctor's surgery.

Author's note. If his doctor's appointment system shared even the slightest resemblance to the one currently being used by my General Practitioner, survival techniques are vital.

'Apparently,' Richard explained, 'all you have to do is to lie face down on the riverbank close to the water's edge, and dangle your arm into the water with the palm of your hand facing upward. The trout eventually become accustomed to your arm being there, they probably think that it's a stick or something, and just use it as cover.'

Fascinated, Andrew said, 'Go on, what do you do then?'

'Well,' continued Richard, 'when the trout swims over your hand you gently stroke its underbelly with your finger. This sort of hypnotises the fish, and you can grab it.'

Innumerable hours were devoted to the pursuit of *Salmo trutta fario* – the brown trout as it is more familiarly known, and the boys quickly learned that their reflexes, when compared to those of their quarry, were painfully slow. One boy fell into the river, not once but twice – on the second occasion slithering into the river like a crocodile that had just spotted its mate on the opposite bank. Andrew on the other hand, seemed to be able to catch fish to order, and often did.

In the true spirit of free enterprise, Andrew regularly sold his 'harvest' to the cook at the big house. This sum, when added to his meagre savings, raised the necessary funds to buy his first guitar. A Watkins 'Dominator' amplifier was later acquired from Minehead Radio at a cost of £5. Andrew fondly recalls that he enquired whether the proprietor of the shop liked to eat trout, but that his efforts to horse-trade were rebuffed.

By the time that he reached his fourteenth birthday, Andrew had been a pupil at Minehead Grammar School for almost three years. Daily practice sessions with an encyclopeedia of chords that he had been given as a Christmas present some two years previously, had seen him blossom into an exceptional rhythm guitarist. In addition, his ability to play most single-note melodies within minutes of hearing the piece meant that he could play lead guitar to an equally high standard. Alone in the kitchen, having completed that day's prep, all that remained for Andrew to do was to write the date on the top page. Glancing at a copy of the *Bristol Evening Post* that his father had abandoned earlier, Andrew noted the date, Wednesday 23 September 1964.

His homework dated and safely stowed in the battered, brown leather attaché case he used for his school course work, Andrew dubiously regarded the newspaper. Quickly scanning the pages, he found little of any interest until arriving at the classifieds, an advertisement immediately caught his eye: 'For Sale: Burns Trisonic electric guitar, good condition, £35. May be possible to deliver.'

Thinking aloud, Andrew muttered 'Trisonic, not bad, and the price is right – I've only got thirty quid to my name, but he might come down a bit.' Minutes later, and deep in conversation with the vendor, Andrew explained that he was £5 short of the asking price, and this before any delivery charge was applied. Andrew finally replaced the receiver with a resigned, 'Oh well, never mind.'

'Problem dear?' asked his mother.

'No mum, not really,' replied Andrew. 'The chap with the guitar said that he'd recently returned from America – wants to go out there again fairly soon, and needs the money for his fare. He did say that he'd be in this area next week, and that he would call in to see if I'd managed to scrape together an extra few pounds.'

'There'll be other guitars, son,' said Andrew's father philosophically.

The owner of the Trisonic called at the Priddy residence late in the afternoon on the following Tuesday. He politely explained that he was unable to lower the price, but that he would waive a delivery charge. He had, he continued, brought the guitar with him in the event of further funds becoming available and, of course, to enable Andrew to inspect the instrument. Andrew reiterated that the sum total of his life-savings was still £30, but agreed to take a look at the guitar. Unlocking the tailgate of his estate car, the man extracted one of two guitar cases, flipped the catches, and looked intently at Andrew, trying to gauge the young man's reaction.

Andrew carefully lifted the guitar from its case with his left hand, removed his right slipper with the other, and placed his foot on to the vehicle's rear bumper. Ensuring that his belt buckle was covered by his jumper thereby eliminating the possibility of damage, Andrew placed the instrument across his right thigh and strummed a few chords.

'It's very nice,' declared Andrew replacing the guitar in its case, 'quite the nicest guitar I've ever played, but that doesn't alter the fact that I've still only got £30. Purely out of interest, what's in the other case?'

Reaching into the car, the gentleman opened the guitar case and said with a smile, 'This is a brand new Fender Stratocaster. Look, the authenticity tags are still on it.'

'Looks great,' said Andrew, 'all right if I have a go?'

'Of course,' replied the man obligingly.

Andrew repeated the anti-damage routine he had carried out earlier before running his fingers over the strings. Caressing the maple neck, he played a chord and gave the tremolo arm a hesitant push downwards.

'It's absolutely brilliant, what a guitar.' Andrew gushed.

'It is nice isn't it?' said the man taking the instrument from him, 'but a little out of your price range I fear. Now then, what about this Trisonic?'

'Oh no,' said Andrew, 'I wouldn't have a Burns after playing that Fender, I'm going to keep saving until I can afford to buy a Stratocaster – how much did you say you wanted for it?'

'I don't believe I mentioned a price, or that I wished to sell it,' replied the owner of the Fender, 'but I would want at least £75 for it.'

'Wait there if you wouldn't mind,' enthused Andrew, 'I'll see if mum or dad can lend me some money.'

He returned within minutes with the news that his parents could only lend him £10.

To Andrew's astonishment, the man rubbed his chin as if deep in thought before saying, 'So with your thirty, you can raise £40.'

'Yes,' said Andrew, still slightly traumatised by the fact that the chap was even bothering to consider it.

'All right,' the man suddenly said, you've got yourself a deal. 'Where's the money?'

Andrew practically floated to his bedroom, the rollicking from his dad and his mother's words, 'You're very silly spending all your savings on a guitar, you won't be playing a guitar when you're thirty, now will you?' a distant memory.

Andrew, with some assistance from his parents, had in fact just purchased a guitar complete with a hard case, for a quarter of the recommended retail price.

Andrew became the rhythm guitarist of a band called the Blues Sect at the invitation of school friend Pete Murphy. Prior to Andrew's recruitment, the Sect comprised lead guitarist Peter, bass guitarist and lead vocalist Brian Jones, and drummer Tony White. The Blues Sect disbanded in 1966 when the four young men left school having played in public on two occasions only, both appearances being at Minehead Grammar School, and both as support band to one of the county's top outfits, The Witness 4. The two end-of-term dances were however sufficient to fire Andrew's love of audience reaction and participation. He had got a 'buzz' from both live performances and wanted more.

Good friend and fellow trout tickler, Richard Hicks, attended public school, and he and Andrew were able to meet during school holidays only. Richard had bought a Burns guitar and amplifier, and he too had learned most of the more commonly-used chords. Andrew's proposal that they form a band, ostensibly to play blues-orientated music, was met with Richard's unqualified approval – until Andrew suggested that Richard trade in his six-string Burns in favour of a four-string bass guitar. His objections were quickly quashed when Andrew picked up his own guitar and began to play. It was evident that Andrew was a superior guitarist in both lead and rhythm departments. Richard subsequently purchased a secondhand Fender Precision bass guitar together with a Vox AC50 bass head, and a Selmer Goliath speaker cabinet. Some years later he had the satisfaction of overhearing Andrew say to one of his guitarist buddies, 'Rich is a red hot bass player, better than I could ever hope to be.'

Drummer Mike Fouracre joined Andrew and Richard as a fourteen-year-old. Talking to a colleague at the Somerset College of Art and Design who played bass guitar with a band in Taunton during his leisure hours, Andrew listened with interest as the bassist 'raved' about a drummer that he had heard that week. 'Honest to God, Andy, he's brilliant. He's a podgy kid, still at school, and he's got this beat-up kit that belongs on a bonfire, but man can he play!' Andrew phoned Richard Hicks that evening, and arrangements were made to listen to Mike's band at a church hall in the Holway area of Taunton at the weekend.

It proved unnecessary to 'poach' the young musician. As the eighteen-year-old lead guitarist of the outfit explained, 'Mike's a good drummer, but he's a bit too young for our band – we're really looking for someone of our own age, but he said he'd stand in until we find somebody.' In less than three weeks the band had found a replacement drummer, and Mike became a member of Justin's Timepiece. Memory fades with the passing of time and neither Andrew, Richard nor Mike can remember who came up with the name.

Richard had passed his driving test and was the proud owner of a Standard 10 motor car. It was in fact his most treasured possession – after his guitar but before his girlfriend – and this, coupled with the Government's steadfast refusal to grant a driving licence to fourteen-year-olds, dictated that practices were held in the Taunton area. The trio was well rehearsed when Andrew spotted an advertisement in the *Somerset County Gazette* which solicited local bands for a talent competition. The 'Battle of the Bands' was to take place on a Sunday afternoon at the Wellesley Cinema in Wellington.

'Shall we enter?' asked Andrew of his two soul mates.

'We stand more chance of winning the British Grand Prix in my Standard,' replied Richard.

'Well I'm game,' said Mike, 'let's give it a go.'

With a completely negative attitude, Justin's Timepiece took the stage at the appointed time – in Andrew's words 'just for a laugh' and played sufficiently well to be declared the best band on the day. Journalist Eric Coombes, a member of the panel of judges and an employee of the *County Gazette* which had sponsored the event, was mightily impressed with the trio and said as much in his column later that week. He was, therefore, not overly surprised when he began to receive telephone calls requesting contact information for the band, and decided to offer his services to the band in a managerial capacity.

Unlike the majority of rock bands who from necessity 'serve an apprenticeship' at youth clubs and village halls before playing at the larger dance halls and theatres, Justin's Timepiece's specialist brand of music catapulted them into the top flight from the outset. The County Ballroom at Taunton, Glastonbury Town Hall, courtesy of local businessman, impresario, and former guitarist Brian Mapstone, where 'Timepiece' was pleased to support, amongst many others, Chicken Shack, Savoy Brown and Fleetwood Mac – at that time a four-piece featuring Jeremy Spence on slide-guitar. They also appeared at the Regal in Minehead, Kidderminster Town Hall (where the band was billed alongside Amen Corner), and the Winter Gardens at Weston-super-Mare where the boys were delighted to appear with John Hiseman's supergroup Coliseum.

In conversation with Andrew Priddy after the Winter Garden gig, drummer John Hiseman was courteous and full of admiration for the young men from Somerset. Singling out Mike Fouracre for special praise, Hiseman opined that Mike was one of the finest young drummers he had heard, and that if he kept playing, he would doubtless become one of the top drummers in the country.

The unexpected success and rising popularity of the band prompted the boys to adopt Eric's proposal that they become professional musicians. The old adage, 'It's not what you know, but who you know' bore a ring of truth when Eric informed the boys that they were to travel to Andover – the home of the Reverberation Record Company, to cut a disc. The resulting disc – a lively song called 'Lonely Man' with an instrumental entitled 'Bull Durham Workout' on the flipside – both of which had been written by Andrew and Richard, sold in huge quantities locally, but was never put on general release.

Eric Coombes (photograph courtesy of the Somerset County Gazette).

A two-week tour of the principality followed the recording session, and Andrew recollects that he, Richard and Mike were on a high for the entire fortnight. The culmination of the tour saw Justin's Timepiece top the bill in Abergavenny – where incidentally, the band had been voted the town's favourite group. Ironically, the support band that evening was an outfit called Love Sculpture, which was currently riding high in the British charts with an instrumental, called 'Sabre Dance'. Andrew recalls that the members of Love Sculpture were slightly miffed to see a huge poster in the foyer emblazoned with the words Justin's Timepiece, below which, in a much smaller font, was the name of their own band. They did, however, have the last laugh. Their fee of £300 compared very favourably to the £35 earned that evening by Justin's Timepiece.

Tours of the Midlands and the North East came hard on the heels of the Welsh trip. Manager Eric Coombes would accompany the trio whenever his working commitments allowed, but was constantly in touch by telephone. On the rare occasions that Eric's presence raised the touring complement to four, lots would be drawn to see which two of the four would spend the night in a nice soft 'Comfy Snuggledown' bed within the confines of a centrally-heated guesthouse or hotel, and which two would sleep in the Bedford Dormobile.

The Dormobile, Richard Hick's current pride and joy resulted from a great deal of haggling with a garage proprietor in Minehead. The chap appeared to be unimpressed by Richard's story – that the Standard 10 he wished to part exchange, was the finest and most reliable vehicle on the roads of Britain today, and seemed to have an aversion to all musicians – reserving a special loathing for 'long-haired yobs that play all this bang, crash rubbish'. Of a certainty, the guitar and amplifier in the rear seat of the Standard did not assist Richard's wheeling and dealing, and probably explains why the Bedford was continually breaking down.

On reflection, Andrew thinks that road weariness affected not only the van, but also the musicians.

'It sounds romantic to be a full-time musician – travelling around the Country, the buzz that you get when an audience is applauding and cheering, working proper hours – instead of nine to five, eating when you're hungry and 'kipping' when you can.'

'But that's just one side of the coin. How about driving five hundred miles when you've only had a couple of hours' sleep the night before – snatching a burger from a 'greasy spoon' café, washing, shaving and changing in the toilets of the club – going on stage and playing for nearly four hours etc. etc.'

After almost ten years together, Andrew, Richard and Mike felt that they had reached the end of this particular road; wished each other nothing but the best, and went their separate ways.

Richard and Mike were to team up again with an outfit called Marsupilami. Andrew took a long break – during which he got married and set up his own photographic business. He was, however, to return to the music scene many years later with a band called Cutting Edge.

Contemplating the interior décor of the gentlemen's toilets at the Barley Mow public house in Rockwell Green near Wellington, teenager Graham Hart glanced skyward and completed his ablutions with a degree of satisfaction – having found what he believed to be a catchy name for the rock group of which he was the lead guitarist. Pointing to the cistern above, Graham said to bandleader and keyboards man Derek Bristow, 'How about that for a name?' Derek carefully studied the legend embossed upon the holding tank, which pronounced that this functional piece of enamelled hardware had been made in England, and was called the Shires Lynx.

'The Shires?' queried Derek dubiously.

'No, you dipstick,' said Graham, 'The Lynx'.

To All Young Lovers Concerned
There is a GRAND SPECTACULAR
VALENTINE DANCE
at the
Blue Horizon Hall
featuring
WELLINGTON'S
TOP GROUP
THE LYNX
on
FRIDAY, FEBRUARY 14th, 1969
from 8 p.m. -- 12.   Admission 5/-
No Admission or Re-Admission after 9.45 p.m.
Cloakroom - 3d
WELLINGTON PRINTERS 3 SOUTH SOUTH STREET WELLINGTON

Born at Bradford-on-Tone, Derek's aptitude for music had first been noticed by his Aunt Nancy Bristow who, together with her husband Jim, ran the little shop in the village of Westleigh close to the Devon and Somerset border. A kindly and Christian lady, Nancy played the harmonium to accompany the Sunday services in the small chapel, and the accordion for amusement and relaxation when at home.

In 1957, when given a mouth-organ as a Christmas present, eight-year-old Derek began the task of learning to play the pocket-sized instrument immediately. His young lungs, unsullied by any substance other than fresh air, were more than adequate to provide almost continuous cacophony for several hours, and an audible sigh of relief from one or two members of the family accompanied the news that lunch was ready. Derek's 'practice' resumed after lunch and continued into the early evening. Unashamedly, his mother Margaret gazed heavenwards and mouthed 'Thank you Lord' when the boy announced that he was quite sleepy and going to bed.

In the following weeks, Derek mastered several tunes on the harmonica – even his sceptical father Jim grudgingly admitted that he recognised most of them. When next visiting his relatives in Westleigh, Derek proudly demonstrated his newly-found skills and happily played a tune for his aunt. Nancy politely applauded his efforts and asked if he would like to try and play her accordion. Derek recalls that the leather cross-straps were shortened with the insertion of a couple of granny-knots and that he could barely see the keys, but he showed just enough enthusiasm and potential to prompt Nancy to suggest that he forsake the mouth-organ in favour of the accordion.

His parents' subsequent purchase of a lightweight, German-built accordion and the boy's daily adherence to a practice regime, spanning many months, allowed Derek to develop his playing style to an enviable standard. The later acquisition of a larger, more versatile accordion manufactured by an Italian company called Fontalini and purchased from a lady in Ilminster at a cost of ten pounds, further improved both his speed and technique. The theory of music and the repetitive playing of the tonic solfa in a number of different keys however, was a different kettle of fish entirely and not at all to Derek's liking.

On Nancy's recommendation, Derek's father had booked a course of lessons with a music teacher called Brenda Drew. An accomplished accordionist, Brenda lived in the picturesque village of Clayhidon some four miles from Wellington. The one-hour tutorials were usually sub-sectioned into four periods of approximately fifteen minutes' duration, which encompassed the rudiments of music, scales, sight-reading etc. As a 'special treat' for her pupils, Brenda would produce the sheet music to a pop song five minutes before the lesson was scheduled to end. Psychologically, this was supposed to relieve the tension and mental strain caused by total concentration on the part of a student who had just spent the best part of an hour getting to grips with words such as fortissimo, crescendo and diminuendo, sharps, naturals and flats.

Following Derek's first lesson, Brenda was puzzled. Sipping at her steaming-hot mug of cocoa prior to retiring for the night, her thoughts returned to the boy who, after struggling with comparatively simple exercises throughout the entire lesson, had played the modern piece effortlessly. At the conclusion of the second session, Derek having once again performed the 'pop tune' without fault, Brenda 'twigged'.

'Have you played these tunes before, Derek?' she enquired.

'Oh yes,' replied Derek, 'I've got the records at home.'

Derek had of course not sight-read the music, but learned the pieces parrot-fashion and indeed, knew a great many more 'tunes of the day'. Much to the annoyance of his parents, Derek confessed that he had no real interest in the theory of music and hated playing scales, expressing the view, 'I don't see the point of taking lessons, when I can learn to play the sort of music I really like from the radio or a record.'

The Lynx at the Community Centre, Wellington. l–r: Graham Hart, Dave Cordy, Chris Heale, Derek Bristow.

The elapse of almost five years found the Bristows resident in Holyoake Street, Wellington. Derek had become a martyr to the delights of coarse fishing, did an early-morning paper round, the wages from which had financed the purchase of an acoustic guitar, and was now a pupil at Courtfields School. Saturdays were reserved for fishing, and it was customary for Derek, schoolfriends Chris Heale and Jeff Newbury, together with five or six others, to meet at Derek's house on Friday evenings to apportion a large quantity of maggots which were to be used as bait the next day. Despite Derek's protestations, his mother Margaret had been adamant that they were not to be kept in his bedroom, but were to be stored in the shed at the bottom of the garden. One particular Friday evening following the share-out, Derek was strumming a few chords on his guitar whilst chatting to Chris Heale. Chris, who had been tapping his fingers on the wall of the shed, idly picked up two short pieces of dowel rod, and began 'drumming' on the metal containers that had until recently held the bait.

'We ought to form a rock group,' said Derek. 'I can play the guitar and you could buy a cheap set of drums couldn't you?'

'I'll think about it,' replied Chris.

In less than four weeks Chris had acquired a 'bit kit' which comprised four drums – each of which had been manufactured by a different company – cymbals, stands and sticks. Fellow fisherman and mutual friend Jeff Newbury had been cajoled into buying a bass guitar, and the hunt was on for a lead guitarist. The search was short-lived: Graham Hart, teenaged lead guitarist and vocalist with established local band Pride had decided to seek a change of direction musically, and when Derek Bristow asked him if he would like to join Chris, Jeff and himself in a new band, he accepted immediately.

Initially, practices were held at Derek's house. Margaret and Jim actually seemed to enjoy the music and were quite relieved that their son and his friends were not hanging around on street corners and getting up to any mischief. Unfortunately, the same could not be said for the Bristow's nonagenarian neighbour Mrs Scott who, under normal circumstances a frail but tolerant lady, took full advantage of the energy-giving and efficacious properties of Philosan, and made her feelings abundantly clear by banging on the wall with the handle of a sweeping brush.

Jeff Newbury decided after just a few weeks that music was just not his forté. Local boy Dave Cordy, who took to the playing of bass guitar immediately, took his place in the band. Following a haggling session the like of which has not been seen outside a Turkish market place, Jeff agreed to sell his bass guitar to Dave. Dave was happy with the purchase, but always wondered why Jeff walked away with a huge grin on his face. Towards the latter end of 1965, the band, as yet unnamed and playing for their own amusement only, were asked to perform before the members of the youth club held at the church rooms and organised by Wellington Parish Church, each Wednesday evening.

The boys began practising in earnest, and were confident that the library of songs and instrumentals they had accumulated was sufficient to see them through. On the morning that they were scheduled to give their debut performance, disaster struck. Apprentice bricklayer and rhythm guitarist Derek Bristow, high up on a scaffold where he had just applied the finishing touches to the pointing of a gable end, heard the very welcome words, 'Oi, Derek, tea-up!' Descending the handily-placed double-extension ladder, the teenager carefully picked his way around the end of the building, turned the corner and slowly walked along the front façade of the new dwelling, nonchalantly tapping the erect scaffold poles and humming to himself as he went.

Derek awoke to find himself in East Reach Hospital at Taunton, his head swathed in bandages and his parents at his bedside. Several wires connected his head and torso to some expensive looking machinery and the occupants of two white coats with similarly-coloured faces stared down at him. He had been unconscious for three days. A four-inch concrete block had been accidentally nudged from the second-floor scaffolding by an unwitting labourer, its passage to the ground only marginally impeded by glancing off the left-hand side of Derek's unguarded (no hard-hats in those days) head.

Three weeks later Derek was discharged from hospital – his guitar proving a useful form of therapy – although because of an ongoing problem with the muscles in his neck, he was not permitted to return to work for almost two months. The discomfort caused by the damage to the tendons at the top of his spinal column resulting from the impact of the concrete block had, both during his hospitalisation and since, convinced Derek that the weight of the guitar around his neck would in later years surely cause a recurrence of the problem, and he resolved to buy an electric organ. The guitar and the Linear 30watts output amplifier were traded in, and a moderately content former rhythm guitarist emerged from a well-known music shop in Taunton the proud owner of a two-manual Vox Continental organ, a Selmer Treble 'n' Bass amplifier, a Selmer Goliath speaker, a five-pound note and some odd change in the pocket of his jeans, and an empty wallet that had earlier contained £450.

The Lynx. l–r: Derek Bristow, Graham Hart, Chris Heale, Dave Cordy, Chris Perrin.

An article in a local newspaper (leaked by lead guitarist Graham Hart) reported that a sensational new band called The Lynx were to appear at the Wellington Community Centre to entertain the employees of the Post Office. The article coincided with the appointment of Chris Perrin as the group's manager, and the outfit gaining a front man. Chris Perrin, an amiable man and resident in Wellington, was no stranger to the band having on occasions given the boys a lift to practices in his Bedford pick-up truck. Acquainted as Chris was with the local music scene, the lads were pleased to have him around.

Rehearsing twice weekly, on Monday evenings at the Community Centre and on Wednesday evenings at the Blue Ball Village Hall, the band developed and improved its existing repertoire, in addition to learning new material which emphasised the distinctive sound of the Vox organ. Vocals had always been slightly problematical. Both Derek and Graham could 'pitch a note' perfectly, but neither felt really comfortable singing the lead vocal lines.

Sitting in the saloon bar of the Sanford Arms in South Street, Wellington, Dave Greedy was in the main happy with his lot. An avid music fan, he had been invited by his friend Chris Perrin to listen to a beat group later that evening. Additionally, Madeleine, nicknamed Midge, the pretty daughter of landlord and landlady John and Wendy Bird, had finally agreed to go out with him. All was well with the world. Dave had just finished his drink when Chris entered the room. Declining the offer of another pint, Dave replaced his empty glass on the bar, politely wished Midge a very good night and followed Chris to his vehicle.

Inside the little hall at Blue Ball, Dave listened intently to the instrumental number that the boys were performing. Turning to Chris Perrin he said,

'They're good, aren't they?'

'Not bad,' replied Chris, 'bit weak in the vocals department though.'

The instrumental ended with a flourish and much cymbal thrashing by drummer Chris Heale, and as if to contradict their manager's opinion, the boys launched into a high energy version of the Chuck Berry classic 'Route 66' – Graham Hart taking the lead vocal on this occasion.

Cupping his hands to Chris' ear Dave shouted, 'Yeah, I see what you mean, they could do with a front man. I think I could do better than that.'

The Lynx. l–r: Derek Bristow, Graham Hart, Chris Heale, Dave Cordy, Chris Perrin.

Approximately three minutes later, and at the invitation of Graham Hart, Dave joined the band on the small wooden stage, opting to sing a number called 'The Letter', a major hit for American vocal/instrumental group the Box Tops. Dave sang the first line of the song to Derek Bristow who quickly established which key he was singing in. Bass player Dave Cordy counted the wannabe singer in with a crisp ' One, two, three, four', and Dave Greedy gave the song everything he had. Graham Hart recalls that he had made up his mind to suggest to the others that Dave be invited to join the band within minutes of his starting to sing. He said as much at the conclusion of the number, and was pleased to find that Derek, Chris Heale and Dave Cordy shared his thoughts. Dave Greedy became the lead singer of The Lynx that evening and remained with the band throughout – his voice playing a major part in the band's success on the local circuit, the Post Office employees being the first to witness the outfit's versatility.

Chris Perrin's entrepreneurial skills were astonishing. Within one calendar month of his taking up the managerial cudgel, he had entered the boys into a local talent competition which was to be held at the Wellesley Cinema in Wellington, accepted a booking for The Lynx to appear at the village hall in Holcombe Rogus, and secured an audition for the television programme 'Opportunity Knocks' for which the group would travel to Bath.

Articles in the *Wellington Weekly News* would subsequently read: 'Exciting new group The Lynx vies with top local band The Pride for first place in talent competition'. And in the Women's Institute column, just below the disclosure that Mrs Wood's home-made damson jam had scooped a highly commended certificate in the club's weekly competition, came the news that members were treated to a good old-fashioned knees-up by five nice young lads from Wellington who call themselves 'The Links'.

The audition for the television programme was nothing short of catastrophic. Chris Perrin had borrowed an old thirty-hundredweight Thames van and nominated Graham Hart as the driver. The journey to the ancient city of Bath was uneventful and completed in good time. Skilfully navigating the one-way system Graham eventually drew to a halt in a narrow road to the rear of the theatre. Peering through the nicotine-stained window in the rear door, Dave Cordy said 'We're OK. There's a sign over there with the word auditions on it.' Disembarking, the boys surveyed the area and saw that the stage door of the theatre was on the far side of a cobbled area, the condition of which bore evidence to the fact that it had undoubtedly been trodden for many hundreds of years. Seizing the initiative Chris Heale said, 'I'll go and have a word.'

A few moments later Chris returned with the information that they were at the correct theatre – that the auditions were running about ninety minutes behind schedule, and that the gear had to be carried a considerable distance.

'The good news, however,' said Chris cheerfully, 'is that the bar's open!'

'Right,' said Graham, 'I'll back up to the door across this cobble bit.'

It is presumed that the smoke belching from the woefully inadequate exhaust system of the van, the slight oil leak, and the fact that the paved area had been designated an area of historic interest, was what incensed the well-spoken but red-faced and very irate gentleman who ran, arms flailing, towards the band shouting, 'Hooligans! Vandals! Tearaways!'

When the equipment had been off-loaded and the City of Bath's self-appointed keeper of the kerbs had been mollified to some degree, Graham drove the van to a nearby car park, walked back to the theatre and joined his friends in the bar. The Lynx took the stage almost two hours later. The number that the boys had selected for the audition was called 'Memphis Train' – the introduction to which required organist Derek Bristow to blow into his microphone, slowly at first then faster such as a steam train might do upon leaving a station.

Derek had huffed his way through the first two bars of the four-bar introduction when Chris Heale's snare drum clattered to the floor. 'Sorry,' said Chris giggling uncontrollably.

'Is it OK to start again?' enquired Graham Hart of a stagehand who looked as alert as a dull five-year-old.

'Eh, oh yeah, well I s'pose that'll be all right,' mumbled the seemingly sedated production assistant.

Graham counted the band in for the second time that day, Derek puffed his way through the introduction, simultaneously dislodging an annoying piece of salted peanut that had hitherto been stuck in a cavity, and Dave Greedy hurtled headlong into the vocal. The Lynx finished the number with a great deal of aplomb, but were not too surprised when they were thanked for attending the audition and excused.

The Lynx at the Wellesley Cinema, September 1976.

Standing outside The Chippery fish and chip shop in Wellington recounting the events that led to The Lynx's non-appearance on national television, Graham Hart and Derek Bristow paused in their demolition of cod and chips to talk to former Courtfields school pal, Ian May. Ian, the son of Chief Petty Officer Vivian Onslow Sylvester, a gunnery instructor in the Royal Navy and Olive May, had moved to Wellington with his parents following his father's decision to leave the senior service.

CPO May, nicknamed Inky, was prompted to leave the Navy after receiving an offer from his brother who owned a gentlemen's outfitters in Wellington. His brother, who traded under the name SAE May, had recently purchased another shop in the town and had offered the business to Inky and Olive. The offer was accepted and Inky, Olive and Ian moved to Somerset. Whilst his parents happily ran their boot and shoe business, Ian was enrolled as a pupil at the primary school in Courtland Road, subsequently moving as an eleven-year-old to Courtfields School.

Young Ian, who was to go through life bearing the nickname Butch thanks to his father's accent (he used to call his toddler son 'my beauts'), had a friend at Courtfields School called Andrew Hawkins. Andrew enjoyed music of all types but held a special affection for brass bands. Keen to learn to play an instrument, he had made up his mind to join Wellington Silver Band. His proposal that Butch also join the band was given due consideration, and resulted in the two boys reporting to the band room for their 'preliminary brush with brass'.

L–r: Dave Greedy, Derek Bristow, Dave Cordy, Chris Heale, Graham Hart, Butch May.

Butch was given a baritone upon which, with much patience, the assistance of other bandsmen and countless hours of practice, he became proficient. He graduated to the euphonium, spending many hours in the company of an excellent musician named Geoff Westcott. The principal euphonium player with the Wellington band, Geoff also played the saxophone and the clarinet. Butch left the band at the age of sixteen when he started his full-time employment. The five enjoyable years that he had spent as a member of the Silver Band came flooding back when Graham Hart, proving conclusively that most guitarists (there are exceptions) could not differentiate between a baritone and a bugle, asked, 'You still blowing your trumpet with Welly Band 'cos The Lynx could do with a sax player?'

Butch recollects that he accepted the implied invitation to join the group immediately, and wandered off up into the town deep in conversation with Graham and Derek Bristow, little details like buying a saxophone, and his fish and chip supper pushed firmly, though temporarily, to the back of his mind.

His 'apprenticeship' with the Wellington town band doubtless helped him to learn to play the newly-acquired £20 saxophone relatively quickly, but surprisingly it was guitarist Graham Hart who taught him the basic principles of rock music and, it transpired, all the wrong fingering. Butch would play a note on the saxophone, keep his finger (or fingers) in position, and wait until Graham had found the note on his guitar, after which the fingering and the note would be committed to memory. Some months later Butch was reliably informed that most saxophones are transposing instruments, which in simplistic terms means that the notes they produce are not the same as the written music. To put it another way, if the keyboards and/or guitars are playing in the key of C, all Bb instruments have to play in the key of D to produce the same notes. Suffice to say that Butch eventually sorted this little quirk out, and became an exceptional saxophone player.

Chris Perrin, nominally employed as a printer, 'worked his socks off' on the band's behalf, accepting bookings and advertising the band's sound and capabilities to anyone who was willing to listen. He located a van almost identical to the vehicle that had given the 'historian' in Bath apoplexy, which the boys bought in a joint venture, and on the rare occasions that he was not employed with 'Lynx affairs', even managed to find time to go to his own place of work.

Brian 'Bert' Huggett, a great friend of vocalist Dave Greedy, was drafted into the band as road manager, and he too played a vital role during the band's time together. Local bookings in youth clubs and small village halls gradually gave way to functions in large dance halls and hotels. The band could be heard at venues throughout Somerset, regularly crossed the border to perform in Devon, and travelled twice annually to Cornwall to appear at the Flamingo Club in Redruth. The Lynx supported many top-flight acts – The Searchers, Pinkerton's Assorted Colours, The Swinging Blue Jeans and Acker Bilk, and were always pleased to accept constructive criticism or compliments from these hardened professionals.

Two major changes to what had become an established line-up appeared to herald the end of The Lynx. Drummer Chris Heale, a hairdresser by profession, regretfully announced to the band that after a good deal of heart-searching he had decided to relocate to Exmouth in Devon. His place in The Lynx was taken by an excellent drummer called Dave Francis, and whilst Chris and his antics – anchoring his drums to the stage at Wellington Football Club with 6-inch nails being one of the more noteworthy – was never forgotten, Dave Francis was a more than adequate replacement.

Author's note. Practices must have been an absolute nightmare for Graham and Derek with three members of the band called Dave.

The other change, although administrative, had a profound effect on the band. Calling the lads together at a rehearsal one evening, Chris Perrin informed them that he would no longer be able to devote his leisure hours to The Lynx. It was his intention he said, together with a colleague, to found an entertainments agency. Local man Rod Wyatt became the outfit's manager shortly after Chris' departure, and did a splendid job for the band during what were to be the swan-song months of The Lynx.

The swinging sixties were all but over when the boys decided to call it a day. It was generally agreed that The Lynx had reached its zenith and, despite the addition of former Avalons vocalist Brian Blackmore to the line-up, the boys felt that they each needed to try something different. The eventual parting of the ways was amicable enough, vocalist Dave Greedy and lead guitarist Graham combined with keyboard player Trevor Bright, bass guitarist Bernie Clark and drummer Clive Cavill to form a band called Tranquillity. After a brief respite, Derek Bristow, Brian Blackmore and Dave Cordy teamed up with former Sabres drummer Pete Stoneley and the ex-lead guitarist of the Pride, Maurice Swithinbank, in founding Salamander.

It is believed that the Selmer saxophone, complete with a hard case, and purchased by Butch May at a cost of £200 during The Lynx's heyday, was consigned to the top of a wardrobe, where it lies gathering dust, but appreciating in value.

PHOTO GALLERY

Sapphire Cabaret Showband.

The Lynx.

Chart-busting visitors to the Westcountry.

Steve and the Bandits.

e Avalons and friends!

ight from Wellington at Blake's Hall,
idgwater.

Charlie Salter being persuaded to get the next round of drinks!

Oasis. l–r: Tony Char-
man, Chris Lane, Sandy
Williams, Steve Orgee.

ocal bass player Dave
tratford (centre) 'depping'
ith Screaming Lord Sutch.

Eddy Dark (second right) and The Salvoes.

Willy's Express at Minehead Football Club.

The Witness 4.

You can teach a young dog new tricks – Lynx keyboard player Derek Bristow's dog, Polar.

The Groups

PART TWO

Monopole in the early days. l–r: Kelvin Brinicombe, Trevor Trevelyan and Rod Cork.

Monopole

The selection of an appropriate name for a rock and roll group has perplexed many a teenager. It is in fact guaranteed to induce more stress than an end-of-term examination. It's so important you see. The outfit's chosen identity has to be interesting, dynamic and meaningful – and obviously not currently being used by any other band.

Born in the village of Westleigh close to the Devon and Somerset border, fifteen-year-old Rod Cork was granted dispensation to enter the bar area of the village pub, the Royal Oak, to watch and listen to a singer/guitarist called Jack Wright. Jack, a basic but adequate guitarist with a fine singing voice often entertained the locals on Saturday evenings, and he and the teenager became good friends. Both during the intermission and at the completion of his performance, Jack taught the young man several of the more widely used chords. These gratis lessons, coupled with a daily practice regime, proved to be extremely rewarding and Rod soon acquired a guitar of his own – a 'Top 20' from a well-known mail order company. In the summer of 1969, Jack Wright's erstwhile solo act was regularly augmented by Uffculme School pupil Rod, who found the experience of playing his guitar in public exhilarating, and a welcome relief from the school curriculum.

Following another 'stunning' performance at the Royal Oak, Rod was approached by a man called Graham Lang who informed him that he wanted to form a group and needed a singer and a rhythm guitarist. Somewhat surprised but definitely interested Rod agreed to give it a go. Arrangements were immediately made for his attendance at the next rehearsal. He was to be collected from his home by the band's lead guitarist Kelvin Brinicombe whose Mum and Dad owned the Domino fish and chip shop in North Street, Wellington.

On the appointed day, Kelvin and his motorcycle arrived punctually at the Cork household and duly sped Rod and his backpacked guitar to the practice session. The rehearsal did not fully live up to Rod's expectations, but he was mightily impressed with Kelvin's guitar work and said as much. Thereafter Kelvin (a multi-instrumentalist having previously played first cornet with the Wellington Town Band) and Rod began practising together. Their joint decision to form a group triggered a chain of events.

Kelvin, fully aware that his motorcycle, whilst fun to ride and a godsend on a hot summer's day, could not be used to ferry him, his guitar and his amplifier to Westleigh, traded the machine for a Reliant Robin three-wheeled motor car, which although spacially challenged, sufficed. A willing volunteer in the shape of Trevor Trevelyan, also fifteen years old and a pupil at

'Celebrating the harvest'. l–r: Kelvin Brinicombe, Trevor Trevelyan, Nigel Thomas, Rod Cork.

Uffculme School, and well known to Rod, was forthcoming with an offer to become the new band's drummer. Two visits to Bill Greenhalgh's music emporium in Exeter resulted in Trevor's, or more accurately Trevor's parents' ownership of a drum kit costing the princely sum of £20, and the Reliant three-wheeler badly in need of a full service.

Rod's aunt, Jennifer Weekes, was coerced into becoming the group's manager on the grounds that, unlike the parents of the three young musicians, she had a telephone. Months of hard work in the practice room (normally Rod or Kelvin's parents' front parlour) and the occasional performance at a friend's birthday party, paid dividends when Jennifer accepted a booking on the boys' behalf, from the secretary of the Sampford Peverell village hall committee. The trio was now in possession of instruments, equipment (albeit one amplifier), a confirmed booking and plenty of confidence. The outfit was lacking only a name! A broken guitar string was to provide the solution…

During a practice session, Kelvin, in an attempt to copy the guitar solo in a song that the band was presently rehearsing, and not realising that the 'sharpening' of the notes in the solo was doubtless achieved with a tremelo arm, many years of practice, or both, enthusiastically bent his second string upwards, creating rather more tension than is normally recommended by the manufacturer, and of course the tape-wound string disintegrated. Philosophically reaching into the side pocket of his imitation leather 'gig bag' Kelvin pulled out a replacement guitar string, made by a company called Monopole!

Rod, Kelvin and Trevor made their debut as Monopole on 27 November 1970 at the little hall in Sampford Peverell, and never really looked back. During the next three years the trio developed musically, and additional equipment was purchased. Adhering rigidly to their policy of a weekly rehearsal, the three boys derived immense pleasure and satisfaction from both these and their occasional live performances.

Late in 1973, Monopole became a four-piece band. Local lad Nigel Thomas had been playing drums for some time, ostensibly for his own amusement although the neighbours did not share in his enjoyment, and he had often wondered whether he was good enough to play with a rock band. Kelvin, Rod and Trevor, having discussed the matter at length, agreed that Nigel should be given the opportunity to do so.

Nigel was in fact a very useful drummer and gelled perfectly. Trevor solved the dilemma caused by the fact that Monopole now had two drummers, when he suggested that he play bass guitar. In theory Trevor's welcome proposal gave the group a more traditional look, and in practice demonstrated his musical aptitude and flexibility.

An audition for the television programme 'Opportunity Knocks' was memorable for a number of reasons. The four young men (they were after all twenty years old now), arrived at the theatre in the City of Bath, and were given verbal instructions and a typed 'running order' by one of Hughie Green's entourage. Hastily setting up the equipment, guitar tunings were checked, and Monopole was ready to perform. The lads listened intently to the first artiste, a young lady with a silky voice who sang a medley of songs from the musical 'South Pacific', and politely applauded as the obviously terrified girl's final notes faded away. 'Thank you,' droned a voice over the in-house public-address system.

Next up was an octet – an eight-piece band that boasted two singers, two guitarists, two bass players and two percussionists, each of whom was resplendent in a 1950s style stage suit, each of which was a different colour.

'They certainly look the part,' whispered Rod Cork to Trevor Trevelyan, 'I wonder if they're any good?'

As if in answer to Rod's question, the band launched into a highly charged rock and roll number complete with a well-choreographed dance routine.

'A bit tasty, aren't they?' shouted Trevor.

The band ended their set piece to a spontaneous round of applause initiated by Kelvin Brinicombe. Fully expecting an encore from the band, Rod and the boys were in no great hurry to pick their instruments up.

'Next!' intoned the unseen voice.

Monopole's hitherto confident air had been unwittingly battered into submission by the previous band, but the urgency and the slight menace in the enunciation of the word 'next', spurred the lads into action. Nigel leapt behind the drum kit, grabbing his drumsticks as he did so; Rod, Kelvin and Trevor picked up their guitars and advanced to the microphones. On the count of four the band started as one – the guitars and drums were perfectly balanced, and a slight grin appeared on Kelvin's face. It was quickly replaced by one of abject horror as he and his fellow vocalists sang the opening line of a Cork/Brinicombe original composition called 'Let's start a Rockin', only to find that the PA amplifier was not switched on.

In less than a heartbeat bass guitarist Trevor turned and flicked the on/off switch. The transistorised amplifier 'fired-up' instantly and Monopole completed the number. The audition director, obviously unaccustomed to public speaking and having a bad day generally, pronounced the 'kiss of death' in his monosyllabic 'Next!'

Certain that the missing 240volts had destroyed their chances of winning the audition but interested to see who had been successful, the boys remained in the auditorium and witnessed the remaining three acts. Convinced that the eight-piece showband were a class apart from the rest of the hopefuls, Monopole were flabbergasted when a 'singing' Jack Russell terrier, accompanied on vocals by a yodelling gentleman with an apparently endless supply of 'doggie treats', took first place. Showaddywaddy, the energetic octet that had preceded Monopole at the audition seemed equally baffled by the result, but gave Spot and his Master a sporting handclap before setting out on the return journey to their home in Leicester. Later that same year, Showaddywaddy went on to win television's 'New Faces' talent competition, and a string of chart topping records followed. 'Opportunity Knocks' was axed in 1978.

Clockwise from centre top: Dave 'Dan' Dare, Rod Cork, Kelvin Brinicombe, Trevor Trevelyan.

Like Showaddywaddy, Monopole achieved success in a talent competition, albeit to a somewhat lesser degree, at the close of 1974. Restricted to local talent, the competition was held at the Wellington Arts Centre and organised by a gentleman called Malcolm Young, an employee of the BBC. A total of twenty acts, solo singers, duos and groups performed before a panel of six judges. Whether memories of the fiasco at Bath pervaded their innermost thoughts is not clear, but upon finishing their allotted two-number set, the boys deftly de-rigged and loaded the equipment into their recently- purchased van.

To their astonishment Monopole was declared the winner. The gear was quickly brought back into the hall, set up for the second time that evening, and the boys happily repeated their act to the delight of the large audience.

Other than playing the drums, Nigel Thomas' consuming passion was speedway. An avid supporter of the Exeter Falcons, Nigel had long harboured a desire to ride one of the gearless (and more importantly brakeless) two-wheeled monsters. In 1974, Nigel achieved his ambition and regularly rode as a novice in the second half of a Falcons' meeting. Rod Cork, also a speedway fan but with no known history of insanity in the family, had no wish to actually ride a speedway bike. Kelvin and Trevor discussed Nigel's exiting from the band at some length. The matter was quickly resolved by Kelvin's suggestion that he play drums. A kit was rapidly acquired and it was business as usual.

Never forgetting their roots, the boys were always happy to accept a booking on behalf of a worthwhile local charity, often performing in village halls such as Hemyock, Churchinford and Culmstock, accepting only their transport costs in payment for their services. Monopole's blend of easy-listening music, instrumentals and rock and roll proved popular with a wide-ranging age group. The band was always punctual, smartly dressed and polite; three attributes which doubtless served to further increase the band's popularity.

The years rolled inexorably by and whilst the trio were content in the knowledge that they always gave of their best, it was the general consensus of opinion that the three guitars and drums line-up allowed for a more expansive and expressive performance than was possible with a three-piece. Guitarist David 'Dan' Dare, a British Telecom engineer from Wellington joined the band for a brief period but found the additional commitment too time-consuming.

John Beer became a guitarist with Monopole in 1976. He had moved to Westleigh from Somerton where, over many years, he had been a valued member of several local bands. Kelvin Brinicombe had heard on the grapevine that John was resident in the village and that he was more than a little interested in forming or joining a group. Having first consulted Rod and Trevor, Kelvin had invited John to join them as lead guitarist. Although John openly confessed his love for Country music he readily adapted to Monopole's varied repertoire, and appeared to enjoy each and every number, as did his new-found friends. John remained a member of the band for almost eight years.

In 1984 discotheques and nightclubs were fast commandeering the available audiences, and Monopole's rehearsals seemed to outnumber the live performances. Kelvin Brinicombe decided that enough was enough, and sadly turned his back on the band that for more than a decade had given him so much pleasure. Rod and John or Rod and Trevor would from time to time play together as a duo, usually in a pub or club. Charitable institutions, local schools and football clubs occasionally requested the services of the band, and where possible these engagements were fulfilled, normally utilising a 'dep' or stand-in drummer.

L–r: John Beer, Nigel Thomas, Trevor Trevelyan, Rod Cork.

In the two previous books in this series which bear the same title, but written in deference to the Rock bands of mid Devon, and Exeter and East Devon, it has been my practice to call a halt to the band's biography in 1980 when, as all we vintage rockers know only too well, music died.

'It went thataway!' l–r: Trevor Trevelyan, Steve Edwards, Rod Cork.

There have been one or two exceptions to this maxim. The band may not have been formed until much later in life but are to this day regularly gracing the boards in the hotels, halls, pubs and clubs of the South West. I might well have been bribed (a £20 note sellotaped to the outside of a quarter-pound of Earl Grey leaf tea would certainly have received my best attentions). Then of course there are the bands that get together once in a while to raise funds for charity, play for three or four hours for a peppercorn fee which barely covers the cost of the fuel to reach the venue let alone return from it, and look for no reward other than to be making music in the company of friends.

Monopole falls into the latter category having assisted Burlescombe, and Holcombe Rogus Primary School as part of the millennium celebrations to raise a substantial sum of money (£900) for two large projects, simultaneously celebrating the band's thirtieth anniversary. Five years earlier in 1995, a Monopole reunion organised by Rod and Kelvin and held at the Beam Bridge Hotel for families, friends and supporters of the band was a huge success, with standing room only by 8.30 in the evening. The pleasure experienced by all those who attended the Beam Bridge on that evening prompted Rod and Trevor Trevelyan to reform the band.

Looks to me like they're playing Apache! Left Rod Cork. Right: Rod Allcock.

Lorry driver Steve Edwards, the father of Connor and Caitlin to whom this book is dedicated, and who, like Rod Cork, worked for English China Clays at their quarry near Westleigh, was recruited to play drums for the 'new' band. Steve, previously the drummer with a Country band called Southern Nights, along with guitarists Gerry How, Martin Sharland and Ken Thomas, had been taught to play drums by Gerry's sister Yvonne Greenslade – the drummer and vocalist with a group called Wildside from Washford near Minehead. Steve's first drum kit, manufactured and distributed by a company called Coda, actually cost 50 pence. No, the author has not omitted several zeroes. A winning lottery ticket purchased at his place of work resulted in Steve receiving the sum of £500 from the promoters.

Much travelled, and a remarkably fine guitarist, Rod Allcock, formerly with two of Mid Devon's top bands, Nashville Skyline from Tiverton, and from Exeter, Gary Kane's Tornadoes, completed Monopole's renaissance.

At the time of writing Monopole can be classed only as a 'hobby band', playing infrequently but with alacrity on those occasions. Rod Cork, Trevor Trevelyan and Steve Edwards are delightful as a trio, and fortunate in that Rod Allcock can be relied upon to lend his considerable talents when the need for a four-piece, bigger-sounding outfit arises. Thirty years on the local circuit and yet they play on. Quite an achievement!

♪ ♪ ♪

The Mustangs

The Mustangs did not follow standards they set them, and along with The Avalons and The Sabres, the outfit was rightly acknowledged as one of Taunton's big three.

Author's Note. I recently had the pleasure of interviewing former Mustangs' drummer Dave Clapperton and I believe that this brief extract from the interview will set the scene for the biography that follows.

Barry: Tell me Dave, other than the love of music, did the lads in The Mustangs share anything else in common?

Dave: Well let's see. All five of us came from Taunton; Charlie Salter, Dave Payne, Richard Harris and myself went to Priory School; Gerry Alexander and I grew up together in Wheatley Crescent. There's two As in each of our names – and finally of course, there's the famous George.

Barry: Sorry, you've lost me. Who's George?

Dave: George isn't a person. The George was our local pub – that's where the band was formed, all the musicians hung out there. There or The Full Moon.

Barry: Gotcha.

Enjoying his own company and a pint of best at a table in the lounge bar of The George public house, Charlie Salter, an apprenticed motor mechanic at Bowerman's Garage in Staplehay, Taunton, was delighted when Richard Harris and his pal Gerry Alexander entered the room and joined him. Some thirty minutes later and alone at the table once more, Charlie reflected on the conversation he had just had with Richard and Gerry, and the fact that he had just accepted an invitation to join a new band that Richard was forming. With a smile, Charlie, the newly appointed rhythm guitarist of Taunton's latest beat group finished his drink and left the pub hoping to catch the last bus home.

From the village of Trull, near Taunton, Charlie, along with fellow villagers Les Warren, Tony and Colin Churchill, and Rod Sparkes, had previously been a member of a little skiffle group called The Grasshoppers, and had often wondered what it would be like to play with a rock and roll band. Employed as a junior clerk at a shirt factory owned by a company called Steel & Glover, seventeen-year-old Richard Harris lived with his parents in Gifford Street, Taunton. Gifted musically he had played the guitar for a number of years and whilst his tastes leaned heavily toward folk/rock, he enjoyed a wide variety of music.

Perhaps best described as reserved, Richard, like Charlie Salter, had played

Three-fifths of The Grass-hoppers skiffle group. l–r: Les Warren, Charlie Salter, Tony Churchill.

The other two-fifths. Left: Colin Churchill, seated: Rod Sparkes.

The original Mustangs. l–r: Dave Payne, Charlie Salter, Gerry Alexander, Richard Harris, Dave Clapperton.

skiffle as a schoolboy with a group called The Cat-Walkers, and although several members of the group had thought his fascination with the work of American singer/songwriter Bob Dylan most odd, they both envied and admired the way that he handled his guitar. He had been inspired to form his own band by watching several local outfits that had sprung up with the advent of rock and roll, and the belief that with practice and the right musicians alongside him, he could do better.

Dave Clapperton subsequently augmented the trio of Richard, Gerry and Charlie. Dave (who had always fancied playing the drums) and Gerry had been friends since childhood, having grown up together in Wheatley Crescent, Taunton. A former schoolfriend of Charlie Salter, Dave Payne completed the line-up. In common with Richard and Charlie, Dave had sung with a skiffle group at school and the move to a rock and roll band had seemed to him to be a natural progression.

The foyer of the Odeon Cinema, Taunton.

Initially, the weekly practice session at Richard or Dave Payne's house was held merely for their own amusement. Charlie's acquisition of an ex-War Department amplifier and the purchase of limpet pick-ups for his and Richard's guitar prompted the rightful owners of the Harris and Payne households to suggest that the lads practised elsewhere. These were duly moved into the YMCA hall where the group was permitted, in the words of Charlie Salter, 'To crank it up a bit'. In addition to the band, there were always one or two friends at the rehearsals, ostensibly to listen to the lads play, but actually because entry was free and it was much cheaper than going to the pub. The number of 'guests' steadily increased to a point where the practice had turned into full-blown dance. Inevitably, one visitor to rehearsals walked up to Richard Harris and asked, 'What's the band called, and how much do you charge? It's my twenty-first birthday soon – I'm having a big party, and I want a group.'

None of the lads can remember who came up with the name Mustangs (Charlie Salter thinks that it may have had something to do with the Ford

Mustang motor car) but the name was adopted by general assent. The gentleman's birthday party led to further requests for their services and The Mustangs' bandwagon snowballed.

The outfit was well established when Gerry and Dave Payne, for reasons unknown, opted to leave. Discussing the matter of a replacement or replacements, Richard and Charlie, having consulted drummer Dave Clapperton, decided that as they both sang lead vocal on many of the songs featured in an evening's performance, only bass player Gerry Alexander would be replaced.

'I think I know just the chap,' said Charlie. 'Nice bloke, name of Mike Green – he was with The Avalons for a while. I think he works for the *County Gazette*. Now I've passed my driving test and got the Dormobile it won't matter if he can't drive. I'll ask him if you like.'

'We'll leave it to you then,' replied Richard.

Mike was indeed employed by the *Somerset County Gazette*. He had studied economics, law and typing at the local technical college, and was now what is colloquially known in the news business as a 'cub' reporter, more correctly, an apprenticed journalist. By the very nature of the job, the work was demanding and occasionally stressful, and he was more than happy to accept Charlie's offer to join The Mustangs. Mike hit it off with Richard, Charlie and Dave from the word go and thoroughly enjoyed each performance, of which there were many. All thoughts of relaxation were dispelled when in the first two weeks of his recruitment, The Mustangs played at Sewer's Hall in Curry Rivel, Blake's Hall in Taunton, the Winter Gardens pavilion in Weston-super-Mare, and a particularly noteworthy birthday party in Milverton.

The birthday party, hosted by the Honourable Mrs Kidd, daughter of Lord Beaverbrook, was to celebrate the coming of age of her son John – better known as Johnny Kidd, who was destined to become an internationally famous showjumper. The day of the party had already been eventful. Richard had decided that hob-knobbing with the aristocracy merited having his hair styled – not cut you understand, styled. The idea seemed to appeal to the rest of the boys, and together they walked to a hairdressing salon in Paul Street, Taunton, called David's. Greeted on their arrival by the proprietors, Elizabeth and David Nash, the lads were soon ushered to their seats and the white protective shrouds deftly applied.

Assuming full command of the situation and addressing the reflection in the huge mirror in front of him Richard said gravely, 'I have no wish to be rude, but before you start, I'd just like to say that most barbers are like sheep-shearers, and I wish to make it perfectly clear that we – that is myself and my colleagues, do not, I repeat do not – want our hair cut like it would be were we at Catterick Barracks!' Richard's solemn speech was duly reported to the *County Gazette*, and a cartoon depicting the lads at the hairdressers subsequently appeared in that most respected of broadsheets the *Daily Telegraph*, on the following Monday morning.

The Mustangs at the County Ballroom, Taunton.

Such was the respect in which The Mustangs were held that the band was approached by a representative of a company called Fenton Weill who, from their premises at Chiswick in London, distributed guitars and amplification throughout the United Kingdom. The representative launched into his sales patter in a manner not dissimilar to that of a street trader in Petticoat Lane, and informed the boys that they had been brought to the notice of his management who had given him authorisation to offer them a superlative deal on amplifiers and instruments, with the proviso that only Fenton Weill equipment was used.

Whilst it was blatantly obvious to the lads that the salesman's interests lay firmly in his commission, Richard quite liked the innovative shape of the guitar he had seen in the catalogue, and the price quoted to replace all the Mustangs' equipment had been very favourable. As was usual in matters of finance, the offer was discussed at some length, and the decision was finally taken to change to Fenton Weill equipment.

In the early hours of the appointed Saturday, having played at Enmore Village Hall on the previous evening, The Mustangs loaded up the Dormobile – resplendent with the band's name picked out in self-adhesive pseudo-metallic fiery red letters – and drove to the factory in Chiswick. Following a late breakfast at a 'greasy spoon' they returned to Taunton mid-afternoon, fully equipped to perform that evening at the County Ballroom on the occasion of the annual Press Ball.

Within just a few hours the boys, dressed in their trademark maroon mohair suits, were on stage. Supporting the celebrated Joe Loss Orchestra, The Mustangs played to an enthusiastic audience of many hundreds whose ages ranged from eighteen to eighty. Charlie Salter glanced at the clock as he climbed into bed and noticed that it was almost 3am. Switching off the light he lay in the darkness and recalled the evening's performance. The Fenton Weill amps and PA system had sounded okay and certainly packed a punch, but he wasn't at all sure about the guitar. Thinking that he'd probably get used to the instrument eventually, he closed his eyes. It had been a very long day.

The weekend following their trip to London was if anything busier than the preceding one. Granted, they did not have to travel hundreds of miles, but they were playing on both Friday and Saturday evening, and on Sunday afternoon. At Nynehead Village Hall on the Friday evening, whilst taking a well-earned break, Richard was complimented on his performance by a chap called Chris Trebble. From Taunton and a mature student at London University, Chris was enjoying a weekend at home, and had been invited to the dance by friends. Thanking him for his comments Richard, who had not been feeling well all day due to an upset stomach, introduced the rest of the band, excused himself and hurried off to the gentlemen's toilets.

To Charlie Salter, Chris said that he thought The Mustangs would go down really well with the Students Guild, and if the band was interested he would strive to get them a booking on his return. Mike Green, never really out of journalistic mode, produced a notebook and pencil from his pocket and wrote down the band's contact details. Thanking Mike very much and nodding to Charlie and Dave, the student wished them a polite good evening and wandered off in search of his friends.

'That's the last we'll hear of that,' said Dave sceptically. 'Get the beer in Mike, I'm going to find Rich, I've got some pills in one of my drum cases that will sort his stomach out!' On this occasion doubting Doctor Dave was wrong on both counts…

A visit to his general practitioner the next morning confirmed that Richard was suffering from gastro-enteritis for which he was prescribed a course of antibiotics, although had he asked, Dave Clapperton would no doubt have had some in his extensive medical kit. Some months later, Mike Green received a letter from the president of the Students Guild together with a contract for the band to appear at the University College of London in Gower Street. True to his word, Chris Trebble had put The Mustangs' name forward to form part of the entertainment at the Annual Summer Ball. It transpired that with the legendary Nat Gonella's jazz band at one end of the huge complex and The Mustangs at the other, a memorable night was had by all. The boys were invited back to the university on many occasions, supporting among others, Dave Berry and The Cruisers, and Herman's Hermits.

The Mustangs cut a record in 1963. Mike Green has the original and only copy. Initiated by a solicitor's clerk from Ilminster called Bernard Pike after meeting the band at the Shrubbery Hotel, the disc was recorded live at another Ilminster hotel, The George. In this year also, Richard, Mike and Charlie decided to once again upgrade the equipment. Out went the Fenton Weill amplifiers and in came Vox AC30s. Richard exchanged his guitar for a Fender Stratocaster, and Charlie Salter traded his instrument for a Gibson

The one and only!

Jumping for joy. l–r: Richard Harris, Charlie Salter, Colin Hayes, Mike Green.

330.   Likewise Mike Green's Fenton Weill bass guitar was replaced by an Epiphone. A noteworthy year was completed when The Mustangs attended an audition at an imposing hall in the Severn Beach area of Bristol. Not only were they offered a Continental tour of the Star Palast chain of clubs, they were also invited to become the backing band for a professional singer from Liverpool called Mark Nicholas.

Neither of these options was taken up. Charlie, Richard, Mike and Dave were content in their present employment, and considered that the Continental tour dates had given them insufficient notice. The lads did rehearse with Mark Nicholas on a number of occasions, but Richard and Charlie thought that the necessary chemistry was missing and the proposed alliance proceeded no further.

Drummer Dave Clapperton left The Mustangs in June 1965 and married his childhood sweetheart, Celia Vickery, a month later. He recalls 'depping' with a couple of dance bands prior to the year's end but gave up drumming shortly after. His position in The Mustangs was filled by local and experienced drummer Colin Hayes who, as Richard Harris so succinctly remarked, 'suited'.

Forris Chance meets a Mustang. l–r: John Forsey, Tony 'Lurch' Elliott, Richard Harris, Charlie Salter.

When founder member, lead guitarist and vocalist Richard Harris left Taunton to live in Paignton, South Devon, it spelt the end for The Mustangs, and although much-travelled and highly talented guitarist/vocalist Pete Bendall stepped into the breech, the band was never quite the same. Under the terms of his contract, Mike was obliged to find other employment upon completion of his apprenticeship. In September 1965 he left the *County Gazette* and joined the *Worcester Evening News*. After only a month in a double-edged bonus, Mike's girlfriend Judy relocated to Bristol and he found employment with the *Bristol Evening Post*. Twelve months later Mike left the Westcountry and moved to Fleet Street in London, working first for the *Daily Mail* and then the *Daily Telegraph* prior to achieving national recognition as a reporter with ITN. At Mike's departure, Charlie, Colin and Pete Bendall decided to call it a day.

Charlie Salter, after a brief semester, teamed up with supremely talented musician and vocalist John Forsey and a guitarist by the name of Tony Elliott, affectionately known as Lurch, in a trio called Forris Chance and remained with the band until John's move to Exeter. As an aside, John Forsey sub-sequently formed a firm and lasting friendship and musical alliance with Richard Harris in a Country duo called Harmony and Slide, which featured Richard on pedal-steel guitar.

Close Harmony. l–r: Charlie, Richard, Colin and Mike.

> *Author's Note. I am given to understand that Pete Bendall currently works and resides at Exmouth in East Devon, and is still involved with the local music scene. Whether drummer Colin Hayes continued in the business following the break-up of The Mustangs is unclear.*

More than forty years have elapsed since The Mustangs entertained the music-loving teenagers of the Westcountry and research has shown that the band is still fondly remembered, especially Charlie Salter's kazoo solo in their cover version of The Coasters classic, 'Along Came Jones'.

♪ ♫ ♪

The chapter entitled 'A Walk on the Westside' earlier in this book bears witness to the huge contribution made by Brian Mapstone to music and musicians in Somerset. His name appears in this biography as the rhythm guitarist, and subsequently the manager, of The Salvoes.

The band evolved from a skiffle group called The Homesteaders. Based in Wookey Hole, the group was formed by Brian together with Mike Argent, Dave Wait and Ian Steinson. The transition from skiffle group to rock and roll band was made with ease. Mike Argent had by this time become an extremely proficient lead guitarist, and the somewhat basic instrumentals by The Ventures, The Fireballs and The Royaltones caused him little difficulty. He invariably played the tunes in the 'as recorded' key but where the fingering proved too tricky, he and Brian were able to transpose the numbers to facilitate easier playing. With only four strings to contend with, Dave Wait usually found a suitable bass line within minutes and, other than being permitted to play louder, drummer Ian hardly noticed the difference. But whilst instrumentals made an interesting interlude during an evening's entertainment, they tended to be boring after a while. The boys were therefore fully in agreement that a vocalist should be found as quickly as possible.

The Homesteaders. l–r: Dave Wait, Mike Argent, Ian Stein and Brian Mapstone.

Born in Old Wells Road, Glastonbury, Ron Fellows suffered from a life-threatening illness between the ages of three and five years old, which left him with a partially-collapsed lung. During his recuperative period he was given a wind-up gramophone and a pile of 78rpm records to help pass the time. Thus, by the time that he commenced his primary education at St John's School some twelve months later, he had memorised the lyrics to songs by the Inkspots, Bing Crosby and gospel singer Mahalia Jackson, and would sing them at the drop of a hat.

In 1957 he was invited to join a skiffle group from Street called Leo and the Lions. The group had been formed by Peter 'Leo' Lee with guitarists Ted Wall, Bill Miller and Alan Tonkins. Drummer Dave Lacey who was later replaced by John, a drummer sharing the same surname, completed the line-up. Thrilled at the opportunity to sing in front of an audience young Ron happily accepted Peter's invitation and resolved to adopt a stage name. After much deliberation, he hit upon the name Eddy Dark – Eddy being a shortened version of his middle name Edward and a derivation of his hero Eddie Cochran's Christian name, and Dark, a reference to his skin tone, which he had inherited from his American father. In deference to their new singer, Peter and the boys agreed to change the name of the group to Eddy Dark and the Cannonballs – this they thought sounded quite dynamic, and more in keeping with a rock and roll band.

Ron stole the show on his first outing as Eddy Dark when he fronted the group at the youth club in Street. He had been with the Cannonballs for almost twelve months when the group broke up, due in the main to Peter and the others commencing full-time employment. Ron was upset when the group disbanded, but he had gained valuable experience and had learned to play a few chords on the guitar, which he considered a definite bonus.

On completion of his secondary education at the newly-built St Dunstan's School, Ron secured employment with Bailey's Ltd, a company dealing in sheepskin products, as a clerk. On hearing via the local music grapevine that a band from Wookey Hole was seeking a lead singer, Ron contacted Brian Mapstone and an informal audition was set up. On the appointed evening Ron rode his Vespa scooter the nine-odd miles to Wookey Hole, and reported to a large room above the village pub, the Wookey Hole Inn, where the band rehearsed. Ron recalls being very nervous initially, but all the lads made him feel welcome and seemed generally happy with his performance. Knowing all of the words to 'Long Tall Sally' and 'Sweet Little Sixteen' were good credentials.

'Look at me when I'm talking to you!' l–r: Mike Argent, Dave Wait, Brian Mapstone, John Lacey and Ron Fellows (Eddy Dark).

After the audition Ron spent a nail-biting ten minutes in the bar downstairs awaiting the band's decision. When it came, it was favourable. He became the outfit's lead singer and front man from that evening, and henceforth the group was known as Eddy Dark and The Salvoes. His recruitment was featured in the local press, and heralded in The Salvoes fan letter – a new monthly publication, produced and distributed by rhythm guitarist and bandleader Brian Mapstone.

This was the spring of 1962. Later in that year supporters of The Salvoes were disappointed when Dave Wait and Ian Steinson made their exit from the band, but delighted with the departing duo's replacements, drummer John Lacey, formerly with Leo and the Lions and the Evenglo's, plus bass guitarist Nick Ponsillo who was 'poached' from Ricky Loxton's Vampires. Vocalist Ron was particularly enamoured with Nick's bass playing, which seemed to complement John's drumming perfectly. With this line-up, The Salvoes exploded on to the pub, club and village-hall scene, throughout South and Mid Somerset.

Fans of the band accepted the changes in line-up without question – John and Nick being given a rousing welcome at their first Salvoes gig in Glastonbury Town Hall. An early booking for Eddy Dark and The Salvoes was as the support band to Gene Vincent and the Blue Caps. Eddy and the boys provided a spirited and wildly applauded set. Eddy's black leather suit, originally chosen as a tribute to the American star, lent real authenticity as he and The Salvoes cheekily played Vincent's hit 'Be Bop A Lula' – Gene Vincent then being second only to Eddie Cochran on his list of all-time greats.

Regular visitors to the town hall at Glastonbury, The Salvoes also double-billed with Dave Dee, Dozy, Beaky, Mick and Tich, Shane Fenton (later to become Alvin Stardust) and the Fentones, the Tremeloes, and Chicken Shack.

Dances at the town hall in the 1960s were not all sweetness and light however. There were many Saturday evenings when the message 'make love not war' went unheeded, and the boys were often witnesses to a pitched battle between rival local gangs. On one particularly memorable occasion Ron recalls observing one such altercation from behind the large frame of 'Ginger' Harris – the epitome of the local bobby! What had started inside the town hall continued outside, ebbing and flowing around the market cross. Thankfully, despite the blatant brandishing of flick-knives, bicycle chains and other makeshift weaponry, there were no serious injuries. Ginger Harris, a cross between Dixon of Dock Green and a brick wall, nonchalantly watched the mayhem from the town hall steps feeling that his decision to await reinforcements from Wells before taking any further action was justified.

The five-piece really hit the headlines locally when they entered a beat competition sponsored by ice cream manufacturer Walls and organised by the Mecca dance hall chain. Successful in a series of heats held at the Locarno Ballroom in Bristol where they triumphed over many fine bands from Bristol and the Westcountry, The Salvoes, as representatives of the Westcountry, were cheered on by three coach-loads of ardent supporters to the regional final in Birmingham where sadly, although lauded for an extremely creditable performance, their dreams of national stardom ended. It is interesting to note that the competition was eventually won by an outfit called The Fortunes who were later signed to the Decca record label, and who almost reached the top of the UK charts in July 1965 with a song called 'You've Got Your Troubles'.

Between sets at Glastonbury Town Hall.

During the next twelve months, Brian Mapstone relinquished the post of rhythm guitarist to manage the increasingly popular Salvoes. For their part, the boys considered themselves doubly fortunate. They had fine representation with Brian concentrating on management, and thanks to Mike Argent's newly adapted block-chord style of playing, there appeared to be little difference in sound quality.

Via the pages of the *Western Press* and the fan club newsletter, manager Brian Mapstone ensured that the positive Walls' experience was well publicised. Not that he had any difficulty in selling The Salvoes. The preliminary heats of the talent competition had brought the band to the notice of several entertainment agents from the Bristol area, all of whom were clearly impressed by the boys who were now based in Street, although one particular agent appeared to have a problem with the group's name – variously advertising the lads as the Savloes, Saveloys and even Savlons.

One of the most respected and popular outfits on the local scene, it came as a surprise to all Salvoes fans when in 1966, due to a disagreement on musical policy, the group decided to call it a day and disbanded. Ron Fellows, alias

Eddy Dark, continued to enjoy a working relationship with manager Brian Mapstone by accepting Brian's offer of employment at Westside Music in Bridgwater, and stayed with the company for seventeen years. Lead guitarist Mike Argent relocated to Weston-super-Mare and joined up with a large show band with which he may still be playing. Bass player Nick Ponsillo moved slightly further north to Bristol but is thought not to have played again.

Undeterred by the break up of The Salvoes, Ron's love affair with music was ongoing. He worked hard at developing his guitar skills to accompany himself, and embarked on a solo career around the local pub and folk circuit. A collaboration with long-time friend and fellow musician Paul Toplis resulted in the formation of a folk-orientated duo called Soft Shoe. In 1978 a long-playing vinyl album entitled 'For Those Alone', a delightful collection of self-penned songs, was recorded creating a high degree of local interest. The disc sold in respectable quantities throughout Somerset and later became a highly prized, and priced collector's item, listed in the Ethnic Punk category.

Author's Note.
At the time of writing, or so I am reliably informed, Ron (now a psychologist) and Pete Lee meet regularly with guitar and banjo readily to hand. Like the man said, 'You can take a musician out of music, but you'll never take the music out of a musician!'

Front cover of the long-playing record 'For Those Alone'.

Arthur Dunn (photograph courtesy of DJ Wheadon).

Born in Taunton, the son of agricultural worker Arthur Dunn and his wife Rita and currently living at West Camel, near Yeovil, Kevin Dunn was immersed in music from a very early age. Arthur played the cornet with the Yeovil Workman's brass band, although he was equally at home when grappling with the multifarious pipework of tenor horns, baritones or euphoniums. As a consequence the limited accommodation afforded by the little tied cottage was, more often than not, further diminished by the storage of one or more of these instruments.

In 1961, Arthur and his family moved to the village of Knowle St Giles, near Chard, where he, knowing exactly where his leisure-time priorities lay, lost no time in seeking out the secretary of the Chard Town Band. That eldest son Kevin would learn to play a brass instrument was inevitable. Arthur quickly tired of having to rebuke the lad with phrases like, 'Kevin! Put that instrument down until you can play it properly,' only to receive the response, 'When will that be, Dad?'

At the age of eight years, by courtesy of a very proud father whose patience apparently exceeded all previous bounds, Kevin was able to both read and play music from a written score to a remarkably high level of competence on either cornet or euphonium, and was subsequently enrolled as a member of the Chard Town Band – as the band's drummer!

The band had placed advertisements in both the local and county newspapers, stating that a percussionist was required as a matter of some urgency, but to date no applicants had been forthcoming. On being assured by the wily bandmaster that no vacancies existed in the cornet, baritone or euphonium sections, Kevin had accepted the post, albeit with feigned reluctance. He thoroughly enjoyed playing the drums, and remained with the band for over seven years. The bandmaster was never to know that Kevin's initial acceptance of the position was due solely to the red sparkle finish of the drum kit. Neither did he discover that Kevin's 'previous experience' consisted of nothing more than banging inverted biscuit tins with a pair of size-nine knitting needles.

Kevin was ten when he acquired his first guitar. His Uncle Dennis had purchased the instrument several years previously, and had had neither the time nor the inclination to learn to play it properly. Gifting the guitar to his musical nephew, Dennis explained that he tuned the instrument to the chord of E, which allowed him to play chords with just one finger. Proving that his musical talents were equalled only by his academic prowess, Kevin successfully negotiated the dreaded eleven-plus examination and became a pupil of Ilminster Grammar School. A popular boy, strengthened no doubt by the fact that he could play half-a-dozen different musical instruments, Kevin mixed well and made friends easily. One of his best friends was a boy called Stephen Hyde. Stephen like Kevin played the guitar and had been born into a musical family: his father Ivor being a virtuoso piano-accordionist and mainstay of the Diploma Dance Band, his sister Anne a pianist and guitarist with a fine singing voice, and a younger brother Phillip, who would attempt to play any instrument that had been left unattended regardless of its weight or value.

Heavily influenced by The Shadows, and Hank Marvin in particular, Steve had previously studied the piano under the eagle eye of a lady called Mrs Mutton, along with his sister Anne, but had soon lost interest, favouring instead the Russian-built guitar that he had received as a Christmas present.

Kevin and Steve hit it off straight away, their combined musical knowledge the envy of many of their classmates. Kevin recalls that Brian Gale, the music teacher at Ilminster Grammar, was a brilliant pianist who was equally at home with classics or jazz, and it was he who suggested that Kevin, Steve and perhaps one or two of their friends, get together in forming a band to play at a forthcoming school concert. Kevin, Steve and a mutual friend named Jeremy Cousins immediately arranged lunchtime practice sessions in the school music room, these rehearsals proving a positive boon when the weather was inclement, or the temperature dropped below zero.

L-r. Kevin Dunn and Steve Hyde.

At the concert, with Steve Hyde playing lead guitar, Jeremy the rhythm guitarist and drummer Kevin using the Chard Town Band drum kit that he had borrowed for the evening, the 'band with no name' took the stage and performed two Shadows' numbers: 'The Frightened City' which Steve maintained was highly appropriate, and 'Genie with the Light Brown Lamp'. To their delight the act, such as it was, met with thunderous applause and encouraging words from Headmaster and local entertainer George Maher; this served to further increase the trio's standing with peers and schoolfriends alike.

Following the concert, Kevin and Steve were keen to keep the trio together, but Jeremy insisted that he was far too busy with both schoolwork and his other extra-curricular activities, and that the evening had definitely been a 'one off' event. The boys accepted Jeremy's explanation without question, but privately thought that as a lover of folk music Jeremy was fearful of the terrible consequences which usually befell rock stars. Kevin and Steve continued to practise together, invariably on Tuesday evenings. Kevin would catch the bus to Steve's house at Wadeford where they would try and play along to the many Shadows' records in Steve's collection. Kevin by necessity had reverted from drums to rhythm guitar using a Vox electric guitar given to him as a birthday present by his mum and dad. The £10 price tag on the guitar would by today's standards be considered a mere drop in the ocean but at that time, the sum represented more than a week's wages for Arthur. After the practice, Kevin would catch the last bus home – and he and Steve would quite literally compare notes at school on the following day.

When, at one of the Coombe St Nicholas Young Farmers Club monthly meetings, of which Steve had been a member for many years, it was announced that a band was required to play at a forthcoming fundraising dance, Steve quickly volunteered his and Kevin's services. His offer was gratefully accepted, accompanied by a generous round of applause.

Sitting in the front room of the ancestral home of the Hydes at Wadeford, Steve and Kevin took stock.

'We can't do this club gig,' said Steve gloomily, 'not just the two of us.'

'We'll have to get a couple of others involved then won't we?' replied Kevin airily.

'Like who?' said Steve wearily.

'How about your brother Phil, he's musical isn't he?'

'Well,' replied Steve, 'he does do a mean impression of Adge Cutler – and Dad did give him a set of bellows from an old accordion when he was about six. He used to stand in front of a mirror and pretend he was playing the accordion, but apart from that, I really don't know.'

'Sounds good enough to me, let's ask him shall we?' said Kevin firmly.

Thankfully, Steve's younger brother Phil, or Bug as he was known to most of his friends, in keeping with the rest of his family, possessed a natural aptitude for music, but a certain amount of nepotistic charm and not a little bribery had to be applied before he finally agreed to become the new band's drummer. Using 'Kevin's' drums, Phil took a crash course in the gentle art of rock drumming – crash being the operative word on many occasions, and within a few short weeks under Kevin's tutelage he was playing like a pro.

At the County Hotel in Taunton. l–r: Kevin Dunn, Phil Hyde and Steve Hyde.

All in all, the Young Farmers dance went as well as could be reasonably expected. The absence of a bass guitarist clearly affected Phil's drumming,

Welcome to the Club. l–r: Phil Hyde, Bob Emery, Kevin Dunn, Steve Hyde.

and Kevin's vocal rendition of classic rock numbers like 'Rock around the Clock', 'Blue Suede Shoes' and 'Johnny B Goode' might well have been better received had they not been of approximately ten minutes' duration each. Nevertheless, Kevin and Steve, with Phil's assistance had fulfilled their promise to the club. A ten-month period of consultation and consolidation followed the club dance. Kevin and Steve had both left school and commenced full-time employment; Kevin joining Chard-based company PJ Engineering as an apprenticed toolmaker, his pal Steve becoming a civil servant.

The band now had a name, Shindig. Taken from the Shadows' instrumental chart hit of 1963, the number was one of the boys' favourites, and had been adopted not only to identify the band, but also as their signature tune. Furthermore, Shindig was now a four-piece. Aware that Kevin and the Hyde brothers were looking for an additional member, local drummer Brian Crouch had introduced them to rhythm guitarist Bob Emery. Bob was recruited without delay, and Kevin became the band's bass guitarist.

Phil Hyde of course was still a pupil at Holyrood School but had now acquired near celebrity status with his classmates, the majority of whom had witnessed Shindig's performance as support act to Somerset's newest professional outfit Stumpy in the school hall. During the next twelve months, Shindig contrived to assemble a varied repertoire, the weekly practices a vital factor in the achievement of this goal, and to create a lasting impression with the public both on and off stage. Initially, bookings were sparse, for which the boys were really rather grateful. Both Kevin and Steve were learning to drive and their driving tests were imminent. Bob Emery was very busy at his place of work, and Phil was currently revising for the end-of-term examinations.

It later transpired that an otherwise perfect year was marred only by Bob Emery's decision to leave the band in search of a new challenge. Kevin and Steve passed their driving tests and were mobile in a Bedford Beagle van and Saab 96 respectively, and Phil was adjudged by his teachers to be slightly brighter than average in his school examinations. This was allegedly due to his extra-curricular and somewhat unorthodox education gained by close contact with strippers and blue comedians at cabaret gigs. Logistics were further improved (by approximately six cubic inches) when Brian 'Willie' Wembridge and his MG Midget sports car joined the band's entourage.

Brian 'Willie Wembo' Wembridge.

In the interest of both accuracy and political correctness, Willie Wembo, the affectionate name bestowed on Brian by the boys, lived at Coombe St Nicholas. He stood 1.9 metres tall, give or take the thickness of a couple of pound coins, (that's 6ft 3in in old money), and was Shindig's biggest supporter in the truest sense of the word. His chief responsibilities were deemed to include the carrying of equipment into and from the dance hall, fetching the drinks, and the speedy retrieval of forgotten equipment. Although when it was discovered that he could sing perfectly in tune, he was appointed guest vocalist: 'Silence is Golden' by the Tremeloes, and Joe Brown's 'Ally Oop' being two of the songs he often performed.

The potential problems caused by Bob Emery's departure proved to be nothing more than a minor inconvenience. Shindig continued for the next couple of years as a rock-orientated guitar, bass and drums trio, although it has to be said that the band's customary signature tune lacked a little something without a rhythm guitar. Normal service was resumed when Dave Ricketts accepted an invitation to join the band. A friend of Kevin 'I can't understand why I didn't think of it before' Dunn, Dave was a drummer with metronome-like timing, and to whom drumming came naturally. Kevin's

Kevin's pride and joy!

brainwave decreed that Phil would become the band's bass player thus allowing Dave to take up residence behind the drum kit, and that he, Kevin, would once again play rhythm guitar. Despite Steve's wry comment, 'Are you sure you still want me playing lead guitar – you wouldn't rather I played harmonica or something?', Kevin's idea worked a treat.

Phil confirmed his versatility, simultaneously demonstrating why he had been awarded a B+ mark for geography in his last examination, by skilfully navigating his way round the long scale bass guitar, and it was merely a case of 'I've been here before' for Kevin as a rhythm guitarist. As anticipated, Dave Ricketts proved first-rate. Quickly acquainting himself with Shindig's library, Dave stayed with the band to the last.

A relatively inexpensive but effective form of advertising created both interest and offers of work. Car-stickers! Self-adhesive and printed upon fluorescent day-glo paper in a particularly tasteless and lurid shade of yellow, the in-car posters bore just one word, 'Shindig'. Given away at gigs, the banners were very popular and the boys frequently received reports that stickers had been sighted in cities, towns and villages many miles from Chard. It is debatable as to whether they would ever have been classified as collectable, but Alan Horne certainly never had occasion to consign one to his cart.

Alan, an employee of the local council charged with keeping the streets of Chard litter free, was an avid supporter of all the local bands and his greatest love was dancing. Resplendent in full 'teddy-boy' attire, athletic Alan (he could dance whilst performing handstands) was the first to arrive at the Chard Corn Exchange on dance nights and the very last to leave. The 'rocking and rolling road-sweeper' was an icon in the area and featured regularly in the local press.

The Rocking and Rolling Roadsweeper from Chard, Alan Horne.

Shindig's simplistic and melodic approach to the music, and the ability to perform in a wide variety of styles, made possible not only by intense rehearsal but by the close friendship and experience cultivated by Kevin, Steven and Phil, when coupled with Dave Rickett's undoubted skills, brought Shindig to the forefront of the local music scene.

The function at the Sidmouth Arms public house in Upottery had been thoroughly enjoyable, the audience was both receptive and appreciative. Pleasantries were exchanged with the locals as the instruments and amplification were loaded into Kevin and Dave's vehicles, and after politely thanking the landlord and his wife, the tired but contented musicians started for home, Steve Hyde riding with Dave Ricketts, his brother Phil the passenger in Kevin's Bedford van. Normally a reliable vehicle, the little Bedford Beagle coughed and spluttered before finally and almost grudgingly firing, by which time Dave Ricketts' Ford had disappeared into the night. Kevin drove slowly out of the car park and had travelled barely a hundred metres when smoke began to issue from beneath the bonnet. Releasing the catch, Kevin gingerly lifted the bonnet to see flames dancing rhythmically on the top of the engine.

'Thumping the door won't make it go now, will it!'

Showing commendable presence of mind, Phil hared back to the Sidmouth Arms, returning a few moments later with a fire extinguisher and a clearly unfit landlord, to see Kevin frantically unloading the equipment on to the grass verge. The small fire was extinguished and the van manhandled back to the pub, where a telephone call was made to Ivor Hyde who, together with a bemused Dave Ricketts, who had been flagged down by Ivor driving in the opposite direction, 'rescued' Kevin, Phil and the equipment. Some months later, another Bedford Beagle belonging to a colleague of Kevin's similarly caught fire en route to the technical college in Taunton. Kevin recalls that he eventually became accustomed to his Shindig colleagues' constant references to the Crazy World of Arthur Brown, and 'Fire'!

With a full diary and constant requests for the band's services, life as a full-time musician was always an option, certainly the lads all felt that they were sufficiently competent to stand shoulder-to-shoulder with the professionals despite the comments of Ivor Hyde who, with his tongue firmly embedded in his cheek, habitually stressed that real musicians sight-read the music as opposed to playing it 'by ear'. But unlike many other bands of the day, 'going pro' was of little interest to the members of Shindig. Indeed, rather than place themselves under any pressure, the four young men jointly decided that after honouring all their existing bookings, they would take a brief sabbatical. Almost thirty years later Kevin, Steve, Phil and Dave continue to take pleasure from this period of respite.

Steve Hyde married attractive former professional vocalist Sally Johnson. Sally, whose parents owned the little shop in Coombe St Nicholas, had joined her brother Bob as a member of a very popular and polished outfit called Venus and Mars, which had enjoyed considerable success on the Continent.

Kevin took great delight in the fact that his younger brother Antony had formed a band of his own, The Phantoms. Born in 1966, Antony seemed

Venus and Mars. Third from the right Sally Hyde (née Johnson).

indifferent to the musical flair of his father and brother, although as an infant he had occasionally 'played' Kevin's drum kit. Apathy turned to enthusiasm in 1980 when at the age of fourteen, he heard American Rockabilly outfit Stray Cats perform their chart hit 'Runaway Boys'.

Antony Arthur Dunn proved to be gifted with the same talent that had been bestowed upon the other male members of his family. Kevin's loan of a temporarily redundant guitar, together with some basic instruction, enabled him

The Phantoms. l–r: Sean Morgan, Steve Barry, Tim Heddington, Anthony Dunn.

Anthony Dunn.

to 'leap-frog' the usual process of saving one's money to purchase an instrument. Having experienced the same passion and emotion towards music, it came as no surprise to Kevin when Antony informed him that he and a few friends were to form a group. The Phantoms comprised Sean Morgan, Tim Heddington, Steven Barry and of course Antony. Practices were held in the shed at the top of Kevin's garden, Antony playing lead guitar, Sean, nominally a six-string player who had been taught by Antony, on bass guitar, rhythm guitarist Tim, and drummer Steve who was also fortunate in that he was able to use Kevin's drum kit.

Kevin recollects that the sounds emanating from the little wooden structure were at best 'rough and ready' but at least the lads were being productive as opposed to destructive. But as time passed, the four young men 'got it together'. The music was tuneful and pleasant although on occasions a trifle loud to Kevin's trained ear. Kevin's unspoken hopes that his younger brother might follow in his footsteps, and that The Phantoms would emulate the achievements of Shindig, modest as they may have been, were dashed on the morning of 5 November 1984. Antony, riding a motorcycle with his friend Paul Morgan as pillion passenger, was involved in a road traffic accident at Staple Fitzpaine and tragically killed; his friend Paul sustained horrific injuries.

Thankfully, and after many months, Paul made a full recovery. The music-loving people of Chard, however, had undoubtedly been deprived of a major talent.

♪ ♫ ♪

The Storm

The following advertisement appeared in the classified section of the *Yorkshire Evening Post*: 'FOR SALE – Lambretta Scooter 125cc. Unwanted gift, fair condition for year. £65 ovno. Will p/x for quality electric guitar'. The advertisement went on to list the contact details for fifteen-year-old John Tingay. John had inherited the scooter from his late father who, together with his family, had returned to his birthplace in Yorkshire from London. During the last few months of his life, John's father required constant care. In an effort to spare the boy further distress, and to give his wife some respite, he issued instructions that John be sent to stay with his long-standing friends, the Parker family who lived in the same village.

John's real interest in music actually began at the Parkers' home when he was asked by Mr and Mrs Parker to hide their son Tony's Christmas present in his wardrobe. John could not resist opening the large oblong box when the occupants of the house were fast asleep. It contained a Hohner acoustic guitar, cream in colour with bright shiny pickups, and John fell in love with it. Carefully replacing the lid of the box, John covered it with a coat, shut and locked the wardrobe door, jumped into bed and was soon asleep.

On Christmas morning he was despatched to his bedroom to fetch Tony's present. 'This,' said John, ceremoniously presenting the box to his friend, 'is from your Mum and Dad. Happy Christmas mate – and if you don't want it, I'll have it!' Tony later discovered that Santa had thoughtfully left a copy of Bert Weedon's 'Play in a Day' under the Christmas tree, and courteously agreed to John's request that they learn to play the guitar together.

At the passing of his father, John and his mother moved to Wellington to live with his grandmother. Born in the Westcountry, his mother quickly adapted to the slower pace of life. Enrolled as a pupil at Courtfields School, John, an intelligent but reserved young man, took rather longer to settle and it was some time before any of his classmates were taken into his confidence. This sorry state of affairs changed with his grandmother's notification that she had submitted the winning entry to a competition in a women's magazine which had been sponsored by a national newspaper.

The competition required all entrants to correctly answer three multi-choice questions, which were as follows:

Q1. Who built the Pyramids? Was it (a) Tarmac Construction, (b) The Pharoahs, or (c) McAlpines?

Q2. Who invented Stevenson's Rocket? Was it (a) Eamonn Andrews, (b) Stevenson, or (c) The Standard Firework Company?

Q3. At what time is the television programme News at Ten shown? Is it,

THE WELLESLEY CINEMA
WELLINGTON
PRESENTS
AN AFTERNOON OF ROCK
WITH
THE LYNX
PHOENIX PRESS
PURPLE RAIN
STORM
AND MANY OTHERS
SUNDAY SEPT 8th 1968
2.30 pm til 5.30pm
Admission 3/-

(a) 2.30am, (b) 5.45am, or (c) 10pm.

She had found the last question a bit tricky. She religiously went to bed at nine o'clock every night and rose at six in the morning, but the lady next door had assured her that the programme came on at ten o'clock in the evening, so she had taken her word for it.

John Tingay.

Her tie-breaker slogan, something like, 'I read the Daily Whatsit because I'm not too good on my pins these days and it's the only one left by the time I get to the paper shop', was adjudged by a panel of lesser-known celebrities to be the best of the three submitted entries. Had John not told his grandmother that he could play the guitar, she would not have entered the competition. The postman delivered her prize, an arch top electric acoustic guitar, personally endorsed by no less a person than Bert Weedon, within a few days of her being officially informed of her win. John was thrilled when his grandmother presented him with the guitar. He was even more delighted when just a few days later he received a letter from Mr Parker enclosing a cheque to the value of £65, in payment for the Lambretta scooter.

At the age of seventeen, John formed his first band, The Blue Diamonds (later renamed The Foot-Tappers), with two friends he had made since leaving Courtfields; guitarist Patrick 'Paddy' Perry and drummer Neil Winter. The Blue Diamonds was in essence a practice band; three teenagers enjoying themselves through the medium of music, with no real future aspirations. Neil was happy with this situation, content in the knowledge that his drumming ability was adequate for a 'hobby band'. It gradually became obvious however, that John and Paddy possessed the ability to progress to the next level, i.e. semi-professionalism, whereas he, in all honesty, did not. Although Neil's stay with the band was brief, he was with John and Paddy at their first paid gig. Following a pleasant if a trifle noisy evening at the church hall in Rockwell Green, Neil formed an orderly queue with his two friends to receive his share of the £1 fee – at that time, the cost of a 45rpm vinyl record.

Sitting in the Poppet Café where he had arranged to meet Paddy, John sipped at his mug of steaming-hot tea and leafed through the latest edition of *Beat Monthly*. Paddy arrived in the company of two other boys, just as he had started reading a very interesting article about The Hollies. Paddy introduced his two colleagues as Robert 'Bob' Conibeer and his brother Paul.

'Bob,' said Paddy, 'is learning to play drums, and Paul wants to sing with a band. I've already told him that you handle all the lead vocal work, but he could have a go couldn't he?'

'Of course,' replied John, 'but what we really need is a drummer. Do you fancy having a bash at it, Bob?'

Bob agreed to join the band on the express condition that he be given ample opportunity to develop his technique, even if that should mean rehearsing on two or even three evenings each week. He rehearsed with boundless enthusiasm and, whilst neither John nor Paddy would presume to call themselves drummers, they were able to help him with his timing, a basic skill, but essential to any band. In addition to the stringent two-evening practice regime, Bob spent many hours in the company of ex-Megatons drummer Tony Paisley who was able to both clarify and demonstrate some of the more intricate drumming patterns.

The band changed its name to The Storm and Terry Rowsell, an employee of Price Bros (now Relyon Ltd) became the outfit's manager. The group also gained a bass player.

In July 1966, Dennis Darch purchased a raffle ticket from a colleague at his place of work. The tickets costing a shilling (5p) each were being sold in an attempt to raise funds for a local charity. When the winners were announced some three months later Dennis was informed that he had won an acoustic guitar. He duly presented the instrument to his highly-delighted thirteen-year-old son Grahame, but warned, 'It'll be bonfire night soon, so learn it or I'll burn it!'

Grahame was fortunate in that Maurice Swithinbank, a friend and fellow pupil at Courtfields School, could play the guitar. With Maurice's help, and constant reference to a chord book that he had borrowed, he beat the 5 November deadline set by his father. Grahame's sister Marlene was most impressed with the speed at which her younger brother had learnt to play. She loved music and regularly visited the Ship Inn in Mantle Street with a few of her friends to listen to The Storm practising. Grahame subsequently attended the next rehearsal with his sister, and was taken aback by the number of people present. John Tingay carried out the introductions starting with Paddy and Bob, and explained that, although Dave Jefferies was not actually a member of the band, he usually sang a couple of songs on practice nights. Terry, he continued, was the manager of the group, and Paul Conibeer was looking to become The Storm's front man. John completed the formalities by introducing Alan Bull and Tony Woolard. 'Alan, or 'Effer' as we call him,' said John, 'is our roadie and he's also in charge of electrics. Tony here has always fancied playing bass guitar, but he doesn't seem able to get his head round it just at the moment.'

BEAT DANCE
at
THE BLUE HORIZON
WELLINGTON

ROCK TO
THE
STORM
Saturday Aug 12th
Admission 5/-
8.00 pm. til 11.45 pm.

Invited to sit-in on rhythm guitar, Grahame had a great time. After the practice session, all three members of the band, who were in truth flabbergasted at the way the youngster had performed, congratulated him. Grahame thanked John and the boys for allowing him to play rhythm with the band, but admitted that he desperately wanted to play lead guitar. Taking him to one side, John told him that lead guitarists were, to coin a phrase, two a penny. 'Bass players on the other hand, especially good ones,' continued John, 'are much harder to find. Take this band for instance, if you could play bass you could join straight away.'

Grahame actually became The Storm's bass guitarist some four months later. His life savings had been withdrawn from the Post Office, and a Burns Trisonic bass purchased from Minns Music in Taunton at a cost of £16. He proved to be a fine bass player and all thoughts of becoming a lead guitarist were forgotten.

Despite Grahame's natural aptitude, the band continued to hold twice-weekly practices using the facilities at the Moose Hall in Post Office Lane when the room at the Ship Inn was unavailable, and the countless hours of hard work finally came to fruition in one glorious weekend. Saturday 12 August 1967 found The Storm playing to a capacity audience at the Blue Horizon in Wellington. Showing no sign of nerves, the lads played their way through a varied selection of numbers that had the dance floor full and the crowd shouting for more. Just sixteen hours later the band was placed second behind Minehead's top outfit Justin's Timepiece, in a beat competition held at the Wellesley Cinema. After the show, in a brief interview with a representative of the local press, Grahame Darch was asked if there had been a particularly special moment during the afternoon. Without hesitation Grahame replied, 'Yep. It was when I found out that The Lynx hadn't entered!'

The Storm. l–r: Paddy Perry, Alan 'Effer' Bull, Paul Conibeer, Bob Conibeer, roadie Merv, John Tingay, Grahame Darch.

The subsequent newspaper coverage of the event was extensive and The Storm lauded for its performance, but the boys were somewhat disappointed that only one confirmed engagement, at Nynehead Village Hall, resulted. Some months later local businessman Alan 'Guz' Garrett replaced Terry Rowsell as manager of the band. A dealer in scrap metal Guz also owned the Ship Inn, knew the group well, and had heard them play on many occasions. Thus he was able to 'sell' the band to prospective dance promoters with a degree of honesty. A shrewd but extremely pleasant character, Guz 'did the biz' for his boys. Due largely to Guz's salesmanship, and within six weeks of his appointment, The Storm appeared at the Labour Club in Taunton, Norton Fitzwarren camp and the Manor Pavilion at Sidmouth in East Devon.

As previously mentioned in this biography, the lads were heavily influenced by The Lynx and, although they relished the fervour and basic simplicity of rock and roll, the addition of keyboard player Keith Jennings turned The Storm into a virtual soul band. Taunton vocalist Mervyn Howell restored the balance somewhat with his Presley covers, but his stay with the band amounted to less than two months.

A telephone conversation between Guz Garrett and a colleague from Dorset gave rise to the most memorable day in The Storm's all too brief history. Having completed the business in hand, Guz went into his well-rehearsed sales-patter on behalf of The Storm. He informed his associate that he now managed one of the Westcountry's top outfits and no, he wouldn't have heard of them yet because the band had been too busy recording. The responsibilities of the gentleman to whom Guz spoke included the procurement of entertainment for The Ritz Ballroom (now the BIC Centre, habitual home to the Conservative Party Conference) in Bournemouth. Later that same week, Guz received a contract confirming The Storm's appearance at The Ritz where the band would support a professional outfit called The Greatest Show on Earth.

The day started badly for the boys and got progressively worse. Other than when they were actually performing, the entire twenty-four hours were an absolute nightmare! It was midwinter and the ambient temperature was below zero. A Bedford Dormobile van and a Sunbeam Rapier motor car towing a small touring caravan left Wellington en-route to Bournemouth at approximately twelve noon. In addition to Keith, John, Paddy, Bob and Grahame, the two vehicles contained Guz, Lurch, Paul and a couple of girlfriends, the caravan being designated solely to the equipment. The boys were within twenty miles of their destination when the Dormobile developed a mechanical problem. On stopping to investigate, it was discovered that a half-shaft had sheared. The proprietor of a nearby garage said that he would be delighted to undertake the repair, but it would of course have to wait until Monday. He was able however to provide the telephone number of a van hire company, and the band was eventually transported to Bournemouth.

Meanwhile, the occupants of the Sunbeam Rapier were also experiencing difficulties. Lurch and Paul, who knew only slightly less than the girls did about the internal combustion engine, had made slow but steady progress, and had reached the pier in Bournemouth just as the engine blew up. When the rest of the party arrived at The Ritz, they were horrified to note that the Sunbeam and the caravan were not in the car park. Hawk-eyed Bob Conibeer finally spotted the recently deceased vehicle with its four-berth attachment on the sea front, and the boys ran down to ascertain the problem. Paul explained that the engine had packed up and that it sounded terminal. All hands were applied to the task of carrying the equipment up to the ballroom and, despite the late arrival, the show began right on cue.

The boys enjoyed The Ritz experience, but the day had been marred by the troublesome transportation. As John Tingay remarked, 'Greatest Show on Earth? They should have called it The Greatest Cock-Up on Earth!' Within days of the Bournemouth fiasco, Paddy Perry announced that he had had enough and was leaving the band. John Tingay too decided that he had other avenues to explore, and the curtain finally fell for The Storm. John did in fact form his own band which he named Dorian Deep, and Grahame Darch, after a break of nearly three years, joined yet another Wellington outfit called Homebrew.

Stumpy (formerly The Concordes)
incorporating The Delta Rhythm Quintet

Slow, Slow, Hic, Hic, Slow...

At twenty-three years of age Ilminster-born pianist Ray Denning should have known better, it was after all the Sabbath day. Granted, it was also his birthday, and he had never tasted rough cider prior to that evening – but to sit at the piano giggling hysterically, well really! A member of The Delta Rhythm Quintet along with guitarist and vocalist Keith Miller, accordionist and vocalist Valerie Pile and her bass-playing sister Pam, and Marwood, known to all as 'Gurney', Slade the drummer, Ray was having a wonderful evening.

The lounge bar of the George Hotel at Ilminster was packed. Filled to overflowing with happy souls, all bent on saying goodbye to the weekend in the time-honoured tradition, with a pint of best and a good old-fashioned 'knees-up'. The locals would probably not have noticed had Ray been completely intoxicated and fallen off his chair, Valerie was a supremely talented accordionist who frequently played the melody line, and was more than capable of camouflaging any minor, or major, Denning error brought about by the innocent if naïve imbibing of a glass of Westcountry champagne.

The Delta Rhythm Quintet. l–r: Keith Miller, Val Pile, Ray Denning. Out of shot: Gurney Slade and Pam Pile.

From the age of five, Valerie was encouraged by her parents, Violet and Alfred, to play the piano. For one of such tender years, and whilst not fully understanding what root notes, thirds and fifths were all about, Valerie had a marvellous memory. She had learned that the white note immediately to the left of a group of two black ones was the note of C, and that when this note was played with two other white notes, an E and a G, she was playing the chord of C. She also knew that this 'play one miss one' method worked if you started on the white note to the left of a group of three black ones, or the white one to the right of that. These were the chords of F and G.

Passing the time of the day with her next-door neighbour while pegging out the washing one Monday morning, Violet mentioned that Valerie loved to tinker on the piano, and that she and Alfred would certainly send her to a professional piano teacher when she was a bit older.
'Has she ever tried to play the accordion?' the neighbour enquired. 'There's a small one indoors that nobody ever plays, she could borrow that if she'd like to.'
'I'm sure she'd love to,' replied Violet, 'I'll ask her.'
Within two years Valerie had graduated to a thirty-six bass accordion, and had become something of a mini celebrity in the local area. Given a few

pointers by accordion maestro Ivor Hyde, Valerie developed her own system of learning songs. Having learned the lyrics, she would pick out the tune with the fingers of her right hand, and then add the contra bass with her left hand.

Valerie first performed in public at the age of seven in the Ilminster Social Club. At this very special evening, a party hosted by the senior management of Standard Telephones to commemorate the closing of their operation at Dowlish Ford, Valerie nervously stood before hundreds of people, and falteringly played a beautiful piece called 'Almost Tomorrow'. The rapturous applause that greeted the final notes of the song brought a huge smile to the youngster's face, and she positively flew through a tune called 'The Happy Wanderer', spurred on no doubt by the audience singing her name in the chorus.

The Harmony Sisters, Val and Pam Pile.

Some weeks later, Valerie entered a children's talent competition held at the Victoria Hall in Crewkerne, and was acclaimed the victor in the 'under 10' section, following her self-accompanied vocal rendition of the Connie Francis hit, 'Lipstick on Your Collar'.

Pam Pile had not been idle during her sister's meteoric rise to fame, albeit in the junior ranks, and had learned to play the banjo, her dad Alfred providing the necessary tuition, and her mum the words of comfort when the tips of her fingers hurt. All thoughts of sore digits were dispelled when Pamela and her sister, in the face of very stiff competition, played through a series of heats held in Bristol, winning on each occasion and claiming the top prize, an appearance on the Carroll Levis 'Junior Discoveries' programme.

The Eaglets skiffle group was formed when an impromptu duet, being performed on the doorstep of number 112 Blackdown View by Val and Pam was interrupted by brother and sister, Colin and Diane Green, neighbours at number 111, who asked if they could join in. Barry Wellman and Des Denning, younger brother of piano-playing Ray, lent weight to the supposition that Blackdown View possessed an inexhaustible supply of musicians, when they completed the Eaglets contingent.

The Eaglets skiffle group. l–r: Colin Green, Barry Wellman, Des Denning, Diane Green, Pam Pile, Val Pile.

All six members of the Eaglets lived within fifty metres of each other, and it is strange that they seemed to drift apart in their early teenage years. They did, however, win a talent competition held at Shepton Beachamp Football Club before doing so, and Val and Pam, who had led the Eaglets from the front, were invited to join The Delta Rhythm Quintet.

Thus, Valerie and Pamela were once again leading by example at the George Hotel on the occasion of Ray Denning's birthday. Ray was not really a drinking man – none of the band was. Shandy or neat lemonade were normally the order of the day, especially when playing to an audience. A traditional dance band that had a lot of fun would adequately describe the quintet. Gurney's favourite trick was to throw lumps of sugar at the audience. No one ever knew why, or presumably cared, but it came to be expected – a kind of trademark. In truth, the strict tempo dance music played by the quintet did not set teenager Keith Miller's pulse racing. He had been playing the guitar, an old Hofner he had been given to him as a Christmas present by his parents, for a couple of years, and saw himself more as a front man, or perhaps the lead guitarist with a rock and roll band. But he did enjoy the company, and thought that the experience he was acquiring would one day come in handy.

In 1965, after five years on the village hall and sporting club scene, Ray Denning came to the decision that The Delta Rhythm Quintet had had its day. Pam Pile had left the band some time ago, her place being taken by Ray's brother Des, and Keith Miller had made no secret of his desire to join an outfit which played music that was less dated. Gurney accepted the demise of the band by philosophically stating that he would save a few bob on sugar lumps. Valerie said that she would doubtless continue to perform, possibly as a solo act, or perhaps as one half of a duo with Pam.

The Concordes.

The new group Ray Denning thought, would encompass the entire gamut of popular music – all the current chart hits, fifties rock and roll, maybe even a little bit of soul. Six months of planning gave rise to The Concordes – Ray Denning selecting the personnel, and his brother in-law Jim Brewer, an engineer employed by British Airways at Filton in Bristol, currently involved with an Anglo/French supersonic aircraft project, supplying the name. Ray had been in constant touch with Keith Miller, and knew that he was keen to get the new band on the road. Keith had suggested that Dave Taylor, a mate of his from Axminster and known in the best of circles as Dilly, should become the band's bass player, which left Ray with just one vacancy to fill. He needed a drummer. Ilminster-based drummer Andy Greer could not have been more delighted at Ray's invitation to join The Concordes had he been mentioned in the New Year's Honours List.

Like a Canadian Mountie on overtime, Ray had got his men. Transporting them and their equipment to practices and gigs would create no problems; he owned a Bedford Dormobile van, but what about the piano? Throughout the life of The Delta Rhythm Quintet, Ray always stipulated that any pub landlord or village hall committee wishing to engage the services of the band supplied a piano. This proviso was usually unnecessary. During the 1940s and 1950s the honky-tonk piano, whether tuned or not, was the keystone of all 'in house' entertainment.

Ray owned his own upright piano, a beautifully veneered piece of furniture that had been in his family for years and was a joy to play, but which could scarcely be described as being portable. Also of course he had the Clavoline. A small keyboard, the Clavoline was the precursor of the synthesiser and is believed to have been the instrument used to give the distinctive 'organ sound' to the Tornadoes chart-topping record, 'Telstar'. Originally designed to be attached to, or used in conjunction with, a conventional piano the Clavoline did not provide the tonal flexibility that Ray was looking for.

A visit to Bill Greenhalgh's music emporium in Fore Street in Exeter rectified the situation. A small cash deposit together with his signature at the foot of a hire-purchase agreement, allowed Ray the freedom to leave the shop with a Vox Continental two-manual electric organ, and an AC30 amplifier, also manufactured by the Vox Company. The keyboard section and the chromium-plated tubular-steel legs stowed in two easily manageable flight cases, thus making the organ eminently suitable for a working band.

The Concordes impacted almost immediately. From the very first rehearsal at the Liberal Hall in Ilminster, the four young men knew that the chemistry was right. Ray Denning, who had collected Dilly and Keith from their respective homes in Axminster and Chard for the practice session and had driven them both home afterwards, parked the Dormobile outside his own house at midnight, and considered that the drive had been well worth it.

All with large record collections and devotees of Radio One and Radio Luxembourg to a man, Andy Greer, Keith and Dilly took little time in building a comprehensive playlist that contained songs which would cater for all ages. Ray recalls that no sooner had one of the three 'boys' thought of a song title, an agreeable key had been found. Then, once the tempo had been set, they seemed to play it quite naturally.

Advertising the band's inestimable value to any likely dance promoter who was willing to listen, was done by word of mouth; Andy and Ray 'preaching' in Ilminster, Keith and Dilly carrying out the same exercise in Chard and Axminster respectively. And it worked! The proprietor of The Shrubbery Hotel in Station Road, Ilminster contacted Ray Denning, and Keith came up with a confirmed booking for the outfit to appear at Chard Working Men's Club. At The Shrubbery, an imposing building and one of the most popular live music venues in the area, The Concordes performed extremely well. With an entrance fee of 25/- (£1.25p), which included a chicken and chips supper, the hotel and its featured band represented good value for money.

The continual badgering of club secretaries in Axminster by a persistent Dilly Taylor eventually had the desired effect. The Concordes were eventually booked by the local Young Farmers' Club to appear at the Guildhall. During the intermission, vocalist and guitarist Keith Miller was approached by a gentleman called Tony Moore. Property developer Tony had for some time contemplated becoming involved in the music industry and thought that The Concordes were worth sponsoring; they were without doubt, the best he had seen for some time. Subsequently, at a meeting held at Tony's home in Axminster, Tony and his wife Frankie enthusiastically put forward their plans for the band's future.

'Clearly,' said Tony, 'the band will have to turn professional – you chaps won't have the time to hold down a full-time job. I shall make sure that you are adequately recompensed, but we can discuss wages later. I think we ought to change the name of the band to something snappy, something less dated. We could run a competition in the local press to find a new name, and award a prize for the best suggestion.'

Cognisant of her husband's continual use of the word 'we' Frankie offered, 'What about your mate in London, Tony, isn't he something to do with Pye records?'

'He's not really a mate, more a nodding acquaintance really,' replied Tony. 'Haven't spoken to him in years, but he might be worth a phone call – the band's certainly good enough.'

Interested, but not yet entirely sold on the idea, Ray Denning suggested that they 'sleep on it' and give their collective decision within a few days.

Ray telephoned Tony the following evening and on behalf of Keith, Andy and Dilly, accepted his proposals regarding the band. Using all of his entrepreneurial skills, Tony initiated a far-reaching advertising campaign incorporating a 'Name the Band' competition. A young art student who had created a cartoon character which she had named Stumpy won the competition, and The Concordes duly became Stumpy.

A company in Exeter was commissioned to manufacture hundreds of toy 'Stumpy dolls' which were to be used for promotional purposes, and agents throughout the South and South West of England were made aware of the new band's existence courtesy of a flyer which announced that the band was currently 'The Best from the West'. Offers of work flooded in.

Keith Miller.

Tony tracked down his colleague in London, a junior executive and talent scout for Dawn Records who promptly arranged to listen to the boys at the County Ballroom in Taunton. Keith recollects, 'Two long-haired blokes and an older chap turned up, and told us that we had to learn to play a particular song.' The song 'Make Me a Superman' was later recorded at the Pye Studios in London, and released on the Dawn Record label as a 45rpm vinyl single. The 'B' side featured a song composed and arranged by Dilly Taylor entitled 'Keep it Going'. Tony Blackburn, Stuart Henry and Simon Dee regularly aired the disc on their radio shows, and many thousands of copies were sold.

> *Author's note. I am given to understand that those original copies of 'Make Me a Superman', record number DNS1080, have become quite collectable. The track can also be heard on a compact disc called 'Glitter from the Litter Bin' – 20 junkshop Glam rarities from the 1970s. On the Castle label, the disc was released on 24 November 2003, and is presumably available from any reputable record store.*

Basically a neat middle-of-the-road outfit, Stumpy slipped easily on to the cabaret circuit. Glam Rock – as perfected by Marc Bolan, David Bowie and The Sweet – became 'cannon fodder' for the comedic talents of Keith and Dilly. Purists would on occasions get more than a little miffed when Keith, resplendent in cut-off jeans that had been dyed bright pink, a sequinned vest and a waist-length white astrakhan fur coat, sang the opening bars of 'Ballroom Blitz', but their anger normally abated when they realised that Keith could actually do justice to the song. Keith's Glam Rock 'fashion statement' did however cause a few eyebrows to be lifted in London.

Tony Moore had signed a contract that guaranteed the band's appearance for fourteen consecutive evenings at The Walkabout Club. Situated beneath one of the capital's larger hotels, it appeared that the club's interior décor had been designed with the specific intention of making Rolf Harris feel at home. Life-sized stuffed koalas vied with aboriginal bric-a-brac for the available wall space. A fully-grown moth-eaten kangaroo that had doubtless, though unwittingly, assisted a taxidermist in paying his mortgage for at least a couple of months, stood on its rear legs holding a placard in its front paws. The sign bore the legend 'Skippy to the Loo', and arrows indicating the whereabouts of the ladies' and gentlemen's toilets.

Stumpy's blend of spoof Glam Rock and easy-on-the-ear music was apparently just the ticket. By the end of week one, Keith, Andy and Dilly gregarious in their nature, had made many new friends among the staff and patrons of the club, and even the normally stoic Ray Denning had adopted g'day as a standard form of greeting.

Following an exceptional performance on the Saturday evening, the boys were invited to an all-night party by a group of boys and girls with whom they had been chatting during the interval. For varying reasons, Ray Denning, Andy and Dilly declined the invitation and retired to their rooms. Keith Miller accepted the offer, and was whisked off by taxi to a flat in the Chelsea area still dressed in the pink cut-offs, fur coat and platform-heeled boots that he had worn during the Glam Rock set which normally closed each Stumpy performance. Keith returned at about four in the morning somewhat the

Saturday Dance

1st March 1975
THE GEORGE HOTEL, ILMINSTER
8.30 p.m. - 12.30 a.m.

Music by "STUMPY"

Ticket 75p.

Stumpy. l–r: Keith Miller, Andy Greer, Ray Denning, Dave 'Dilly' Taylor.

worse for wear having travelled by tube, bus, and shanks's pony barefoot, from the south to the West End of London. A person (or persons) unknown delivered his high-heeled stage boots to the hotel later that day. Keith rose from his bed at midday and steeled himself for the inevitable inquisition by the rest of the band. Strangely, the subject was barely broached, Dilly it seemed, had had 'problems' of his own.

Apparently the bass player had said goodnight to Ray and Andy after the previous night's show, and had been standing in the corridor of the hotel, rummaging through his pockets for the key to his room, his guitar leant against the door, when a rather effeminate gentleman clad only in his boxer-shorts and with a towel wrapped around his head, appeared in the doorway of the room opposite, and asked him if he could borrow his hair-dryer. Obligingly, Dilly agreed to the request and having located his key let himself into the room. Returning from the bathroom with the hair-dryer, Dilly was surprised to see the fellow sitting on the edge of the bed admiring his guitar. Immediately invoking the guitarist's law 'Take my wife, take my life, but leave my guitar alone!' Dilly politely asked the man to put the bass down.

'Oh don't worry dear,' the man said, 'I'm in the game too.'

It had been a long evening, and Dilly wondered momentarily if he had heard the man correctly, did he say in or on? Not wishing to be unduly rude but very tired, Dilly said, 'You are?'

'Yes,' replied the man, 'I used to play drums with a pro band called Blood Sweat and Tears.'

Handing over the hair-dryer Dilly quirkily ended the conversation with, 'Well, perhaps you'd like to beat it to bed, I'm bushed!'

Promising faithfully to return the dryer in the morning, the man offered his thanks and left the room. Dilly locked the door and went to bed.

Keith recalls that Stumpy's last night at The Walkabout Club was a real party affair, and that the band was treated like royalty by both management and

G'Day from The Walkabout Club.

staff. 'It was great,' said Keith. 'Andy Greer got it right when he said bookings like this are what makes it all worthwhile.'

Back in the comparatively quiet Westcountry the bright lights of London were soon forgotten, and whilst the Perry Street Club near Chard did not perhaps have the same allure as The Walkabout, the boys very much appreciated the fact that the good people in their local area thought highly of the band; they were after all, paying their wages.

Some years later Tony Moore severed his links with the band due to the pressure created by the high-level projects he was currently involved with but Stumpy, at this time South Somerset's only truly professional outfit, were extremely marketable and dance promoters and agents alike continued to bombard the outfit with engagements. Stumpy became an international act courtesy of entertainment's agent Don Jones who, from his office in Bournemouth, represented some of the top names in the world of light entertainment. His telephone call to Ray Denning offered the boys the opportunity to undertake an all-expenses-paid tour of Denmark. The four-week tour was scheduled to commence in three weeks' time, and the agent wanted an aye or nay pronto!

Andy, Keith and Dilly were thrilled at the prospect, but Ray had severe misgivings. Qualifying his concerns Ray said, 'It's bad enough when things go pear-shaped in this country. Lord knows what we'd do if we had problems thousands of miles away!' Thirty minutes later Keith Miller rang Don Jones and informed him that Stumpy would be pleased to accept his offer and that all further communications should be addressed to him.

Ray Denning walked away from Stumpy fully believing that he had made the right choice. He had wished his three friends the very best of luck in the sincere hope that they would achieve the success that they so richly deserved. Talking to Valerie Pile later that week, Ray mentioned that he was no longer a member of Stumpy and enquired whether she was still playing. Valerie said that she and her sister Pamela had formed a vocal/instrumental duo called the Harmony Sisters, which seemed to be quite popular locally. Reminded by Valerie of the fun times with The Delta Rhythm Quintet, Ray mused that it might be nice to return to the dance band scene – he would give some thought to the matter. After a self-imposed break of almost twelve months, Ray teamed up with saxophonist George Waits and his trumpet-playing son Paul, to form a dance trio called The Paul Ray Sound.

Keith Miller meanwhile was 'getting one of his heads'. He had that day received the itinerary for the Danish tour and noted that Don Jones had efficiently tabled the tour dates, venues and playing times, accommodation and fees. Further scrutiny of the document had revealed that passports, work-permits, ferry tickets and such were the sole responsibility of the band. There was also the little matter of logistics. With the departure of Ray Denning, the band was presently without adequate transport, and lastly, the contract clearly stated that Stumpy would tour as a four-piece. With a heavy

At *The Shrubbery in Ilminster.*
l–r: Ray Denning, Keith Miller,
Andy Greer and Dilly Taylor.

heart Keith reached for the telephone, it was going to be a long day.

In the event, Keith's day proved to be less problematic than he had first thought. Andy Greer and Dilly both held a current British passport, an antiquated Ford Transit van was found at a garage in Chard and purchased at a reasonable cost, and he had eventually traced keyboard player and guitarist Phil Crick to his new address in Dunkeswell and invited him to join the band.

At the age of eight and on the insistence of his father Richard, affectionately known to his friends as Dick Crick, Phil had taken piano lessons from a certain Miss Madge, a music teacher who lived in Chard. A multi-instrumentalist, he played the violin, piano, clarinet and saxophone with equal ease, Dick had taught, among many others, the renowned organist Peter Scriven to play the violin. He steadfastly refused however to teach his son to play the piano, preferring to sub-contract the task to another.

Phil did in fact take very few lessons with Miss Madge, and recalls that the first, and last, set piece that he played in her presence was a tune called 'Bobby Shaftoe'. He did however exercise his natural musical ability on an almost daily basis using the piano at home, and found it uncommonly easy to pick out virtually any tune that came into his head – a talent that did not go unnoticed by his father. At the age of twelve Phil was presented with an old harmonium that his father had bought for 10 shillings (50p). Dick was flabbergasted a few days later when he heard the boy playing Russ Conway's latest chart-topper 'Side-saddle', and once again raised the subject of professional tuition. Phil explained to his father that he wasn't really interested in keyboards of any description, and would much prefer to play the guitar.

Whilst very much a classical musician, Dick appreciated the fact that his son was a lover of music, although he had his doubts as to whether skiffle and rock and roll could ever be described as such, and acceded to Philip's request that he be allowed to buy and learn to play the guitar. Like many boys whose parents could not, or would not, finance the purchase of a top-of-the-range guitar, Phil bought an inexpensive Spanish round-holed instrument. The successful mastery of the guitar subsequently prompted Phil to buy a Watkins Rapier solid-bodied electric guitar and a little 10watts output amplifier. Thus, on meeting guitarist Keith Miller at Holyrood School in Chard, he found that they shared a common interest.

In the early days Phil occasionally played with The Delta Rhythm Quintet, his first gig with the band being at the Memorial Hall in Tapworth near Chard, where he struck up an immediate friendship with accordionist Ken Dudderidge. He later joined a band called the Toppers, this time as a bass guitarist. The Toppers comprised four members of the Matthews family namely, Mum and Dad and their two sons Brian and Michael, and a chap called Tom, a trumpet player who lived at Awliscombe, near Honiton. Phil fondly remembers that Dad Matthews' principal function within the band was to turn the pages of the sheet music for his piano-playing wife, and to keep her supplied with boiled sweets.

Phil formed a band called Ricochet when he left the Toppers, but the group was short-lived. Thus the telephone call from Keith had arrived like a bolt out of the blue. Phil had of course heard of Stumpy, there could be few in the area that had not, and relished the thought of standing alongside three very accomplished musicians. He also rather liked the idea of touring Denmark having travelled no further than Bristol previously.

Phil slept badly that night but had reached a decision by morning, and telephoned Keith Miller at 7am. At 8.30am he reported to Express Dairies in Honiton where he was employed as a laboratory technician, and informed his manager of his intention to quit at the end of the following week. By mutual agreement, and the sacrifice of some of his accrued holiday pay, Phil was able to leave the company just two days later.

Stumpy rehearsed solidly for the next eight days at the end of which Phil was fully au-fait with the band's library. Beginning at 10am, the practice sessions at Carnaby's Club in Yeovil normally wound up at around 6pm. On the Thursday evening, two days before the band was scheduled to sail from Harwich to Esbjerg in Denmark, Keith Miller received a telephone call from agent Don Jones…

'Hello Keith, it's Don Jones.'

'Oh, hi Don, what can I do for you?'

'Well, I've just been speaking to an old pal of mine. He runs a youth club called the Four Feathers in Bayswater, and he needs a band from 8 o'clock until 11.30 tomorrow night. I thought you boys might fancy doing the job as you're heading in that general direction. He'll put you up overnight, and you can toddle on up to Harwich on Saturday morning.'

'Yeah, that'll be fine Don, tell your mate we'll be there, I'll ring the boys now.'

Keith collected Dilly and Phil from their respective homes about twenty minutes later than specified, having spent a little longer than anticipated at Andy Greer's house. By way of an apology, Keith said that he had been assisting Andy in the trans-shipment of ten one-gallon plastic containers of rough cider, from his car to the van.

'So what's with the cider then, Andy?' asked Dilly.

Andy explained that he doubted very much whether the Danes had ever tasted anything like it before, and he might be able to sell it to them.

'It'll probably get us locked up,' muttered Keith, 'or them!'

COMBINED SERVICES
ENTERTAINMENTS
PRESENTS
THE
BAY CITY ROLLERS
&
THE WEST COUNTRIES
LEADING
SHOWBAND
STUMPY
PLUS
BILBO BAGGINS
APPEARING
AT
AKROTIRI
THURSDAY AUGUST 12th 1976
7.30 pm til 12.00

The boys reached Bayswater at three o'clock and located the Four Feathers without difficulty. The club warden greeted them on their arrival, and asked one of his colleagues to keep an eye on the van whilst he showed the lads to their dressing room. 'Parking,' he explained, 'is a nightmare around here.' He pointed at a black and yellow striped barrier that appeared to be guarding the cellar of the large building opposite. 'There's a car park over there, but it's a private job for the staff of the Insurance Company that owns the offices above. There are security guards on duty twenty-four hours a day, close-circuit television cameras and it's locked between the hours of 8pm and 8am.'

'Sounds just the job,' said Andy Greer. 'Why don't you boys start unloading the gear. I'll go and have a word with the security bloke.' He returned a few minutes later, took a gallon of cider from the rear of the van and retraced his steps to the car park. When Andy finally returned, he said with a grin, 'I've just done a deal with the security guy. I swapped him one gallon of cider in exchange for one night's parking.'

The scrumpy, although it had turned green since its collection from the farm in Ilminster, appeared to have travelled amazingly well and proved to be very popular with the Danes. Sitting on a park-bench in Esbjerg enjoying the sunshine and a glass of cider, Andy and Phil struck up a conversation with three local lads who had been at Stumpy's gig the previous evening. Andy politely offered each of them a glass of cider, and to his surprise they loved it! The afternoon's pleasantries ended with Andy and the three youths exchanging five gallons of cider with twenty cases of Elephant Lager – a product of the giant brewing company Carlsberg, with whom the young men were employed.

During their mini tour of the Kingdom of Denmark, and in addition to their five-day spell in Esbjerg, the boys played to capacity houses in the cities of Arthus, Aalborg and the Danish capital, Copenhagen.

In January 1977, having won a series of heats in Bath, Bristol and Plymouth, Stumpy reached the televised stages of the Thames Television talent show 'Opportunity Knocks'. Often criticised for promoting acts that were at best mediocre, the show nevertheless played a vital role in bringing fresh talent to the notice of the public. In the studio, Stumpy's performance pushed the 'clapometer' to the limit and the boys were declared the winner by the show's genial host, Hughie – 'I mean that most sincerely folks' – Green. In the postal vote, however, Stumpy was beaten into second place by a singer called Berni Flint. Berni's debut single, 'I Don't Want to Put a Hold on You' entered the UK charts in March of the same year. The song peaked at number three, and remained in the charts for ten weeks.

The band's appearance on national television gave rise to a spate of enquiries and confirmed engagements. A summer season in the 'Pig and Whistle Bar' at Butlins Holiday Camp in Minehead preceded hotel work throughout the winter. Happy to spend the Christmas and New Year period with their families, the boys were back on the road in early January.

And so it continued. Stumpy was placed first in a talent competition held at the Webbington Hotel and Country Club; the band was singled out for special praise by a panel of judges that included Angie Bowie the wife of superstar David. To the winner goes the spoils, and on behalf of the band Keith Miller accepted a large gold-plated cup that was later engraved with the name Stumpy, and which was described by Phil Crick as a pretty useless bit of kit!

Stumpy enjoyed many memorable experiences during its time at the very top of the local tree: a trip to Cyprus when the band was flown from RAF Brize Norton to support the Tremeloes at the RAF station in Limassol, and the numerous occasions when the boys performed for the workforce on an oil platform in the middle of the North Sea to name just two.

None of the boys can remember exactly why or when Stumpy disbanded, but it is known that the band played well into the 1980s.

The Volcanoes

Until quite recently, I confess that I had little or no idea as to the location of Donyatt, other than that it was in Somerset. In a rural setting, the village lies just a few miles to the west of Chard on the A358, boasts a population of approximately 300, a small shop and a pub, but has neither cinema nor youth club. In past years, however, Donyatt featured a pottery and four volcanoes among its attractions...

In the late fifties, teenagers Peter Bealey, Peter Knight and John Summers, all from Donyatt and pupils at Ilminster Secondary Modern School, decided to form a skiffle group. The combined financial resources of the trio being at a premium, Peter Knight thought it might be possible to acquire a set of plans and make a pair of guitars. 'We'd have to buy the necks,' he said, 'but they shouldn't cost the earth.'

L–r: John Summers, Dave Beck, Pete Bealey.

'Well,' replied Pete Bealey, 'my pocket money can be put towards some wood, or a set of strings, my father doesn't play his banjo much these days, I can whip the neck off of that.'

Scavenging expeditions to the sheds of family and friends resulted in the accumulation of sufficient timber and plywood to enable Peter Knight, with some assistance from Pete Bealey, to build two round-holed acoustic guitars. Frankly speaking, the construction, symmetry and overall look of the two instruments were never going to cause commercial manufacturers a great deal of nervous tension or insomnia, but it was possible, after annealing the fingertips of the left hand by regularly immersing them in malt vinegar whilst lazing around at home, and with much gritting of the teeth, to play basic chord shapes as depicted in guitar maestro Bert Weedon's esteemed publication, 'Play in a Day'. John Summers was elected to the post of tea-chest bass player, and the foundations of what was to become an extremely popular, semi-professional rock band had been laid.

Dave Beck.

Upon leaving school, Pete Bealey became an apprenticed blacksmith, working in the neighbouring village of White Lackington. Peter Knight gained employment with South West Farmers Ltd at their retail premises in Donyatt, and John Summers was indentured as an apprentice electrician with Horlicks Dairies in Ilminster. Within hours of commencing work at the dairy John had met Dave Beck. Dave, originally from the Ilminster area, had recently moved to Donyatt with his mother Irene and lorry-driving father Bill. The total absence of leisure opportunities in the village figured heavily in conversation between the two young men, Dave commenting that he frequently cycled to Chard to visit the cinema or youth club. Nodding sagely, John said that he too had previously travelled to Chard or Ilminster for entertainment, but from the moment that he and a couple of his mates had formed their little skiffle group, village life had become decidedly more tolerable, and he was thoroughly enjoying his 'home-spun' music.

'I've got a guitar,' said Dave…

The guitar in question, a present from his parents and several decades old, was innately similar to the Knight/Bealey custom model in as much as most of the glue that held it together had perished with the passage of time, and the neck remained secured to the body by God's will alone. But Dave could play it. He very quickly brought himself up to speed with the group's modest repertoire and practised at home on a near daily basis.

The Ploughboys skiffle group. l–r: Mike Giles, Dave 'Bunny' Singleton, Pete Bealey, John Summers, Peter Knight, Dave Beck.

It was whilst strumming and humming in the front parlour of his parents' house in Crock Street one Saturday morning, that the baker's van arrived, from which Derek Baker, the son of Mr Baker, the baker of Ilminster, dispensed bread and cakes to the inhabitants of the many outlying villages in the area. Accepting Dave's offer of a cup of tea, Derek enquired as to how long he had been playing the guitar. Some forty minutes later, having fleetingly mentioned that he had often fancied playing drums, a bemused roundsman left the Beck residence well behind schedule, and newly recruited to the skiffle group.

When combined with the three acoustic guitars and the tea-chest bass, Derek's initial purchase of snare drum, stand and sticks created just enough noise to prompt the reverend gentleman who lived in the rectory immediately forward of the Old School House in which the band rehearsed, to suggest that they practise elsewhere. Thus Crock Street, courtesy of Irene and Bill Beck, became the new rehearsal venue for the Ploughboys – the identity chosen by the boys from many suggestions.

They were to face an audience in this guise on just two occasions. The first, at the mid-year church fête in the village of Ilton, for which an advertisement in the local newspaper read 'Grand Summer Fête, stalls, sports, music and pony rides (if wet, in the Village Hall)', proved a rip roaring success, and gave the young musicians much encouragement. The second and final, 'live per-formance' saw the Ploughboys cast into the script of the annual pantomime at Donyatt. Such was the importance placed upon this engagement by the skiffle group, that new cravats were purchased for the occasion.

During the next two years, Pete Bealey, Dave Beck and Pete Knight purchased pickups for their spanish guitars which, when plugged into the back of a valve wireless, reel-to-reel tape recorder or radiogram, sounded to the untrained ear more or less like the guitars used by their heroes. John Summers invested in a 'brand name' bass guitar made in Hong Kong.

John's acquisition of a 'proper' bass appeared to fire the enthusiasm, and/or envy, of Dave Beck and the two Petes who, by the end of 1959, had taken his example to heart and also bought modern instruments. In a frenzy of spending, matched only by the January sales at Poundstretcher, ten watts output practice amplifiers followed the purchase of the 'new' guitars. Derek

Baker, who by this time had assembled a full drum kit which although not particularly pleasing to the eye was perfectly serviceable, was coming under increasing pressure to devote more of his time to the family business. An open and amicable discussion with the other members of the band regarding the wishes of his parents enabled Derek to leave the group in a much happier frame of mind.

A young man called Peter Baulch took Derek's place in the band. Aware of the little outfit's existence, having on many previous occasions spoken to Dave Beck at a youth club in Chard, Peter, the son of a local haulier, accepted Dave's current invitation to join the group. An arrangement that Peter purchase Derek Baker's drums was made to the mutual satisfaction of both parties, and rehearsals continued much as before, Peter taking to percussion like a caterpillar to cabbage.

Rock and roll had taken a stranglehold on both the British and American charts, and Pete Bealey was keen to add items from this new and exciting genre to the band's library. He also felt that the name Ploughboys was somewhat dated, and that it did not adequately reflect the frantic pace of modern-day music.

'What we need,' he said, 'is a name that's explosive, and screams hot rock at you – like a volcano!'

'Getting their act together.' l–r: John Summers, Pete Knight, Pete Bealey, Dave Beck and Peter Baulch.

Skiffle became music of the past. Cover versions of songs by Eddie Cochran, Gene Vincent, Chuck Berry, Elvis Presley and Jerry Lee Lewis, with Pete Bealey and Dave Beck sharing the duties of lead vocalist, condemning classics like 'Freight Train', and 'It Takes a Worried Man', to the far reaches of the mind.

The band was thrust into the limelight at the end of 1961 by Chard musician and impresario Frank Huddy. An accomplished organist in his own right, Frank promoted his own dances and would whenever possible give new, and especially local talent, the opportunity to 'strut their stuff' in front of a live audience. Frank's offer to the boys, a one-hour rock and roll spot during the intermission at his next function, was greeted with mixed emotions.

'Who's the main band?' asked Pete Bealey.

'The Modernaires,' replied Frank. 'They're a good dance band, but they don't play much rock and roll.'

'Oh,' said Pete Bealey.

'When is it?' muttered Dave Beck.

'A week next Saturday. That's November 18 at the Corn Exchange in Chard,' replied Frank anticipating the next question.

'I'm not sure if we're ready for this,' said John Summers nervously.

'We'll do it!' said Pete Bealey.

'What about some sort of uniform?' said Pete Baulch.

'We'll still do it!' said Pete Bealey.

The speed at which the band 'got their act together' was remarkable. Pete Bealey paid an unannounced but nonetheless welcomed call upon his Aunt Hilda Larcombe. A kind and softly-spoken lady, Hilda worked as a seamstress at a factory in Chard that manufactured shirts, and was always very pleased to see her nephew… Well, nearly always. To her eternal credit, Hilda managed to 'run-up' five lightweight stage jackets, red in colour with black Italian-style lapels, for the boys in the group. At the time of writing, Hilda Larcombe is ninety-three years young and well remembers the 'flashy coats'.

Jim Knight.

Peter Knight's chosen task involved nothing more complicated than to say to his elder brother Jim: 'Hey Bruv, any chance of you dropping me, the rest of the boys and the gear into Chard on Saturday week, we've got a gig?'

Originally from Taunton, Jim Knight and his family had moved to Donyatt via Winscombe near Weston-super-Mare, and the village of Horton. Called up for National Service in 1947, Jim joined the Royal Air Force and served in both the Middle and Far East. Following his demobilisation from the RAF he returned to the butchery trade, once again employed by Mr Britten, the proprietor of a butcher's shop in Silver Street, Ilminster, for whom Jim had worked at weekends whilst still a schoolboy. Deliveries forming an integral part of the quality service offered by his employer, it had been necessary for Jim to pass his driving test. Thus it was that he was able to assist The Volcanoes with his six-seater Morris Oxford estate car, in the unfamiliar role of road manager.

At the Corn Exchange, the newly booted and suited Volcanoes, playing rock and roll to a predominantly middle-aged audience, rose to the challenge and gave a competent, if nervous performance. At a debriefing session following the function, Frank Huddy congratulated the lads on their presentation. The audience's reaction he said had been heartening. Furthermore, he continued, the band had arrived punctually, been well dressed on the stage and that he would have no hesitation in re-booking them. Standing slightly to the rear of the promoter, changing from stage-wear into travelling clothes, Pete Bealey gave the thumbs-up sign to Jim Knight and mentally thanked his Aunt Hilda before saying to Frank, 'Where do we go from here then?'

'Home I should think,' replied Frank shrewdly, 'it's gone midnight now.'

Frank subsequently signed The Volcanoes to his 'Double H' entertainment's agency, and to date maintains that the band was one of the most reliable, and indeed marketable outfits on his books.

The Volcanoes at Donyatt Village Hall.

Engagements at Ilminster, Bridgwater Town Hall and the Guildhall in Axminster followed hard on the heels of the band's 'premiere' at the Corn Exchange. Pete Bealey began to receive requests for the band's services from club secretaries and dance promoters and these, when added to the seemingly incessant traffic from Frank Huddy, meant that to have a 'gig free' weekend was a rarity.

Jim Knight appeared to enjoy the occasionally arduous duties of roadie equally as much as the boys enjoyed performing, and in truth, was not looking forward to the day when the lads passed their driving tests thereby potentially rendering him surplus to requirements. With the assistance of his youngest brother John, Jim produced some wooden signs bearing the legend 'The Volcanoes Beat Group', together with the telephone numbers of both Pete Bealey and Dave Beck. Sized to fit the side and rear windows of the Morris Oxford, the vehicle itself was responsible for several enquiries.

Whilst performing at the Guildhall in Axminster as the support band for Shane Fenton (later to be reincarnated as Alvin Stardust), and the Fentones, the secretary of the Shand Engineering Social Club, situated immediately behind the Guildhall, drove into the club's car park and heard the sound of a rock and roll band. Thinking that the outfit would be well received by the members of his own club, he walked towards the front of the Guildhall in an attempt to ascertain the name of the act. Passing the stage door on the side of the building, the secretary encountered Jim's Morris, noted the contact numbers, and telephoned Pete Bealey the following morning. Pete Bealey often wondered whether it was The Volcanoes, or the Fentones that the club secretary had heard that evening, but was happy that as a consequence, he and the boys were booked to appear at the social club on many occasions.

The evening at the Guildhall was made doubly momentous by the presence of a gentleman called Brian Davis. A talent scout for Weymouth-based agent and promoter Howard Lock with a rapacious appetite for music generally, Brian haunted theatres, clubs and halls, in search of dance bands, beat groups, and cabaret artistes that had not hitherto featured on the East Devon or Dorset circuits. Arriving at venues incognito and working to stringent criteria, Brian vetted each act and submitted his report to Howard during the next working week. Thus the Weymouth promoter was sure that any act finding its way on to his books was there on merit.

It was a delighted Dave Beck who conveyed the gist of Howard Lock's telephone call to the other members of the band. 'A guy called Howard Lock,' he proudly announced, 'has booked us to play at Seaton, Salisbury, Yeovil, Dorchester and Weymouth – we're topping the bill on a couple, and playing support act to some pros at the rest. He didn't have time to tell me all of them, but he did mention Sounds Incorporated, and some bloke called Big Dee Irwin.'

Busy as they were by virtue of the contract with Howard Lock, The Volcanoes tried, whenever possible, to honour any engagement offered by the HH agency. 'The job's at Lynton Town Hall on New Year's Eve,' Frank Huddy had said. 'I haven't been able to get the fee I really wanted for you – but the guy's a mate of mine; I'll waive my commission, and they're having a buffet so you'll get fed, should be an easy night.' Drummer Pete Baulch had elected to leave his little Austin A35 at home. He had been stopped by the police a week earlier following a Christmas dance at Curry Rivel Youth Club, informed that one of his rear lights was not working, and issued with a warning. He had apologised to the police officer, and explained that the lights did on occasions seem to have a mind of their own. Walking to the rear of the vehicle, Peter had raised his eyes to the heavens, muttered 'Let there be light', and kicked the off-side wing, whereupon the lights had obligingly burst into life. Unimpressed with the drummer's impersonation of a Kwik-Fit fitter, and showing a distinct lack of Christmas spirit, the constable had growled, 'Faulty wiring, get it sorted!'

Sitting in the front seat of Jim's roomy Morris, Pete was apprehensive. Dave Beck and John Summers, aware that Peter was a notoriously nervous passenger, had been at pains to extol the view from the top of Countisbury Hill. 'It's a sheer drop down into the sea,' John had said. 'But you can see for miles.'

'D'you think Jim's bus'll make it up the hill?' Dave had asked, rather enjoying Pete's obvious discomfort.

'Shouldn't think so,' John had replied gleefully, 'we'd better follow in Pete Bealey's Jowett, that way we can always get out and help push.'

Readers familiar with the topography in this picturesque area of Somerset will realise instantly that Dave and John had conveniently omitted to inform Peter that on the outward journey, the abyss in question would in fact be a considerable distance away, and on the driver's side of the vehicle.

The journey to Lynton was of course incident free, Jim's trusty Morris Oxford negotiating Countisbury Hill without manual assistance, although Jim well remembers Peter shifting uneasily in his seat in an attempt to put even further distance between himself and the Bristol Channel. On their arrival at Lynton the boys were not a little surprised to be greeted by a gentleman formally dressed in a dinner jacket with matching accessories.

'You do know that we're a rock and roll band don't you?' said Pete Bealey to the function organiser. 'I mean, look at your guests, they look like they've come straight from the set of 'Come Dancing'!'

Assured by the host that all would be well, but filled with foreboding, The

Volcanoes started to play. To the band's amazement, the dance-floor rapidly filled to capacity; chiffon and satin cut swathes in the air as the ladies whirled, and bow ties and dinner jackets were quickly consigned to the backs of chairs. The chimes of Big Ben rang out from a small-transistorised wireless at midnight, and the boys sang 'Auld Lang Syne'. Hugs, kisses and best wishes for the New Year were freely exchanged, and The Volcanoes were happy to be included in the merriment. The net – strung high overhead and containing dozens of brightly-coloured balloons – steadfastly refused to part with its contents on cue, only doing so at two in the morning as the guests were departing, but a wonderful night was had by all. In deference to his passenger, Jim took a different route back to Donyatt on the homeward journey, stopping just once to purchase a bottle of milk from a milkman on the outskirts of Taunton at 4am.

In January 1963, Pete Bealey received a telephone call from the entertainment manager of the Blue Waters Holiday Camp in Seaton, East Devon, requesting the services of The Volcanoes for the forthcoming twenty-six weeks' duration summer season. Already very busy, the band discussed the offer at length prior to signing the contract.

'Hi De Hi!' The boys at Blue Waters Holiday Camp.

Doubtless one of the most popular acts to appear at the holiday camp, the band was contracted for three years consecutively. Interest however was waning. Peter Bealey was soon to be married, and the strain of performing on four, or sometimes five, evenings each week whilst 'holding down' a full-time job, was visibly affecting both Pete Knight and John Summers. When Peter Baulch left the band to join his father's transport company, The Volcanoes disbanded.

Pete Bealey promptly became embroiled in the thrills and spills of wedlock, Pete Knight and John Summers devoted their excess energies to their 'real' jobs, and Dave Beck, after a break of almost a fortnight, teamed up with local musicians Godfrey White and Des Denning in forming a Country band called the San Antones – from which evolved the highly successful and very popular Denver Spur.

Willy's Express

Cruising through the streets of Minehead at four o'clock in the morning in his battery-powered milk float, Dave Buckley glanced at a notice in the window of the Red Lion Inn: 'Under new management! Old and new patrons welcome. Good food and a selection of fine ales. Live music on Fridays and Saturdays.' It was the last bit that interested him!

Formerly the rhythm guitarist with a Manchester band called The Thin Red Line, he had recently relocated to Minehead to take up the offer of employment with a local dairy. Dave enjoyed a pint of beer, but to date had been too busy to find a regular watering-hole due to essential internal refurbishment of the cottage that formed part of his milkman's salary.

Sitting at a table in the bar of the Red Lion the following Saturday night, listening to an organist who was currently doing a severe injustice to a medley of Lennon & McCartney songs, Dave took in the convivial atmosphere, and his thoughts turned to his days with the band back home in Manchester. His train of thought was interrupted by a polite, 'Excuse me. May I join you?'

The man sat down and introduced himself as Bill Hadley. As the evening progressed the conversation deepened, and the two men discovered that they were very similar in many respects. Born in Minehead, Bill had moved to a place called Bedfont, between Staines and Hounslow, at the age of eleven, and moved back to Minehead some thirteen years ago. Soon after his return to Somerset, he had joined popular local band, The Witness 4, replacing well-known guitarist and vocalist Pete Bendall.

Within a very short time, Dave and Bill had formed a duo called Strings Electric and were themselves performing at the Red Lion on one evening each week. Essentially an instrumental duo (Shadows' tunes were relatively easy to play and there were lots of them), Bill was persuaded by a very large young lady to sing a love song to her even larger friend. His unrehearsed rendition of Elvis Presley's 'Are You Lonesome Tonight?' was followed by cheers, the stamping of feet and sustained applause. It also earned him a hug from the larger of the two young women, and he vividly recalls thinking, whilst enveloped in the lady's enormous bosom, that the ability to breathe through the ears would be most advantageous.

The moderate success of Strings Electric during the first twelve months prompted Bill Hadley to suggest that the duo be augmented. Drummer Tony White accepted Bill's invitation to become a member of the new band, and he was joined by Minehead restaurant owner and keyboard player, Bob

The Thin Red Line at Audenshaw Royal British Legion Club in Manchester. l–r: John Chilcott, Lance Homer, Barry Turvin, Dave Buckley.

The Witness 4.

Strings Electric. Left: Dave Buckley. Right: Bill Hadley.

Bass player Tony Charman with Karl 'Kung Fu Fighting' Douglas.

Davies. Having replied to an advertisement placed in the *Somerset County Gazette* Tony Charman, originally from London where he had been the bass guitarist with 'The Big Stampede' the backing band of Karl 'Kung Fu Fighting' Douglas, but now resident in Taunton, attended a rehearsal held at Bob's restaurant, and was duly offered the job. Now officially a five-piece band, Bill and Dave decided that Strings Electric needed a new name.

As the non-singing half of Strings Electric, it had befallen Dave Buckley to introduce any vocal number that was sung by the other half of the duo, namely Bill. Dave would inform the audience that he was proud to introduce Minehead's answer to Shakin' Stevens, Wobbly Willie, whereupon Bill would launch into a song called 'This Ol' House'. Without a drummer to set and control the timing, Bill invariably sang the number far too fast, rather like an express train in fact.

Doodling on a serviette in Bill Davies's restaurant, Dave wrote, 'Willie's Express'. All manner of thoughts pervaded his mind as he stared at the two words. He grinned as he quickly scribbled through both. He wrote again, 'Willy's Express'. Smiling broadly, he passed the serviette to Bill Hadley and said, 'How about that for a name?'

Rocking at the County Ballroom in Taunton.

Well rehearsed and smartly dressed, with an extensive library of vocal and instrumental numbers, it is perhaps a little surprising that it took almost two years for the band to become fully established. Bookings appeared to be limited to sports clubs, social clubs and hotels in the immediate vicinity of Minehead. Dave recalls a dance at Wellington Football Club as being the band's first 'out of town' gig. For his part, Bill Hadley recollects that on receiving a telephone call confirming the Wellington booking, he rang Tony Charman with the news that the band was 'going on tour'. Bill had just cause to remember the event for many months after...

As was their normal practice, the boys travelled to Wellington in four cars; Dave riding with Bill, Bob Davies, Tony White and Tony Charman in their own vehicles. Bringing his car to a halt in front of the football club, Bill left Dave to unload the contents, and strolled across to Bob's Ford Granada Estate. Together with Bob he wrestled the two-manual organ from the rear of the vehicle, uprighted the instrument, and carried it bodily into the function room. As they were lifting the organ on to the stage, the heavy wooden lid fell, hitting Bill squarely on the head. Resisting the temptation to check the condition of the lid, Bob suggested that Bill apply a cold-compress to his head. The band played particularly well that evening which led to Tony Charman's post-function comment that Bill ought to be 'banged on the bonce' more often!

The remaining members of Willy's Express were not unduly concerned when, after approximately fifteen months, Bob Davies left the band to concentrate on his restaurant business. The line-up of lead and rhythm guitars, bass guitar and drums tended to be traditional, and was perfectly adequate for rock and pop music.

The band came to the fore thanks to the antics of some youths from the Midlands who were holidaying in the Dawlish area of South Devon. Bill Hadley had accepted the booking at the Grand Hotel in Dawlish without reservation; it had after all come from Ginger Walker, the well-known and respected entertainment's agent from Tiverton. On arriving at the 'Grand', Dave Buckley surveyed the fast-decaying exterior of the hotel. 'D'you know,' he said to Tony Charman, 'I went to Coventry when I was a lad, and I saw buildings that had been bombed by the Luftwaffe in the Second World War which were in better nick than this place!'

Tony did not reply immediately. He appeared to be mesmerised, or in a state of shock. Turning to Dave he blurted out, 'My God! Bill and I have booked in here for the night, what sort of state are the bleedin' bedrooms going to be in?' Their opinion of the hotel was reinforced when they entered the lounge bar. The barman seemed to be suffering from terminal lethargy, but was gracious enough to put his newspaper down in order to indicate the door leading to the function room. Tony Charman wanted to go home there and then, but Bill Hadley insisted that they honour the engagement. 'You never know,' said Bill, 'it might be a good night, we've played in worse places haven't we?'

L–r: Tony Mirando, Bill Hadley, Tony Charman, Dave Buckley.

Both Tony and Dave Buckley were unusually quiet whilst the equipment was being unloaded and set up. Sound checks were completed and the boys went out to the bar for a drink before playing. They were pleased to note that a healthy crowd had assembled. 'Told you so,' smirked Bill, 'we're in for a lively night.'

At eight o'clock precisely the boys launched into their first number. Their audience gradually filtered into the room from the bar, and slowly but surely the tables that encircled the dance-floor were occupied. The dance-floor was as deserted as a Baghdad beach-hut for almost three-quarters of an hour, although the audience looked and sounded happy enough. Bill had been happy to sing the only Jim Reeves number he knew for an elderly gentleman who had responded with his thanks, and the offer of a drink. Bill had accepted both gestures gratefully and watched as the old chap stopped at his table, helped his wife to her feet, and walked towards the bar, never to return. Willy's Express called an intermission at ten o'clock, and resumed the performance twenty minutes later.

Dave Buckley recalls that it was 11.20pm when a group of youths wearing kiss-me-quick hats, obviously the worse for alcohol and in varying stages of undress, came into the room and onto the dance-floor. Their singing, although the word is used in its loosest sense, flailing arms and legs, whilst not particularly menacing, certainly inhibited the dancing of other patrons. The pleasant atmosphere that the band had built during the evening dissipated almost immediately, and several people decided that it was an appropriate moment to leave.

Bill Hadley's polite request that the adolescents have some consideration for

With yet another change of uniform! l–r: Dave Buckley, Bill Hadley, Bob Jarvis.

other dancers was largely unheeded. When one of the youths staggered onto the stage, grabbed a microphone from its stand and started to sing during one of the band's quieter numbers, Bill finally lost his self-control. Taking the drunken individual firmly by the forearm he marshalled him off the stage. As the boy stepped off the low platform he aimed a roundhouse punch at Bill's head. The guitarist neatly side-stepped the blow and delivered one of his own. He repeated the exercise with two of the youth's associates, and Dave Buckley joined the mini-fracas by handing out a lesson in manners to a fourth. Drunks number five and six decided to err on the side of caution, and meekly followed their colleagues out of the room. As the band restarted the number that had been so rudely interrupted, a spontaneous round of applause rippled around the room…

After the function, the boys were treated to several drinks by the management of the hotel who had had problems with the unruly juveniles earlier that week. As he and Tony were preparing to embark on the sixty-odd-mile journey back to Minehead, Dave Buckley turned to Bill Hadley and remarked, 'You know what you were saying about playing in worse places. Well, I can't think of one!'

Quite how the press got hold of the story is unknown, but headlines like 'Willy's Bring Express Relief to Intimidated Dancers' featured in many South Devon newspapers. Ginger Walker received a flurry of requests for the band's services, but was quick to point out that dealing with drunken louts did not normally form part of the group's contractual obligation. Thankfully, the incident was a one-off occurrence.

Willy's Express was an amenable and pleasant sounding outfit. Blending contemporary with traditional pop music, the boys wanted only to entertain. Personnel changes during the lifetime of the band were few and always attributable to the drummer and/or the bass player. There were in fact only three drummers who could claim to have been permanent members of Willy's Express: Tony White, Brian Howe and Tony Mirando.

In 1984, bass guitarist Tony Charman opened a music shop at East Reach in Taunton, and set up his own recording studio – MTM Music. He quickly discovered that his leisure time was at a premium. Many of the acts that wished to avail themselves of the comprehensive facilities at MTM enjoyed semi-professional status, and as such were free to record in the evenings and at weekends only. Tony left Willy's Express in the summer of that year, taking with him the best wishes of Bill, Dave and drummer Tony Mirando.

A period of uncertainty followed Tony's departure. Steve Bothwick, a first-rate and much in demand bass guitarist acted as a stopgap prior to joining the entertainment on a cruise liner, and Bob Jarvis, former bass player with Pure Gold, the Hotspots, and the Ginger Walker Band, carried out a similar exercise in his stead. 'BJ' was with Willy's Express for over twelve months, and it is fair to say that he would certainly have been part of the outfit at its swan-song had he not relocated to Exeter.

The band's final line-up of Bill Hadley, Dave Buckley and drummer Brian Howe, together with bass guitarist Bob Walder and Dave Ackroyde, a guitarist with amazing skills who had been recruited to pave the way for Dave Buckley's intended exit, continued to provide entertainment of the highest quality until 1986.

A Band of Absent Friends

Jack Chard – Organist – Homebrew.

Colin Churchill – Tea-chest bassist – The Grasshoppers.

Tony Churchill – Guitarist – The Grasshoppers.

Dave Cordy – Bass guitarist – The Lynx and The Salamander Showband.

Iain Davidson – Drummer – The Jaguars and The Generation.

Peter Knight – Guitarist – The Volcanoes.

Ian Lucas – Guitarist – The Beatmakers.

Bob Patey – Organist – The Beetones.

Dave Payne – Vocalist – The Mustangs.

Tim Poole – Guitarist – The Popeyes, The Germs and The Somerset String Ensemble.

Chris Sayer – Vocalist and Guitarist – The Ravens, The Germs and The Somerset String Ensemble.

Ray Thyer – Drummer – The Crusaders.

Sadly there may be more – but their memory is nevertheless honoured here.

© David 'Dan'' Wood